JESUS
C E O

Laurie Beth Jones

HYPERION   New York

JESUS
C◦E◦O

Using
Ancient
Wisdom
—— *for* ——
Visionary
Leadership

"Gardener" © 1992 reprinted by kind permission of Ann North. "Midnight Stars" © 1993 reprinted by gracious permission of Irene A. Jones.

Library of Congress Cataloging-in-Publication Data
Jones, Laurie Beth.
    Jesus, CEO : using ancient wisdom for visionary leadership / by
Laurie Beth Jones.
        p. cm.
    ISBN 0-7868-8126-7
    1. Success.   2. Success in business.   3. Jesus Christ — Leadership
style. I. Title.
BJ1611.2.J64   1994
158'.4 — dc20   94-20680
                                                                        CIP

Designed by Claudyne Bianco

First Paperback Edition

20 19 18 17 16 15 14

Contents

STRENGTH OF ACTION ❧ 79

STRENGTH OF RELATIONSHIPS   175

APPENDIX ❧ 293

Preface

Jesus, CEO: Using Ancient Wisdom for Visionary Leadership is a practical, step-by-step guide to communicating with and motivating people. It is based on the self-mastery, action, and relationship skills that Jesus used to train and motivate his team. It can be applied to any business, service, or endeavor that depends on more than one person to accomplish a goal, and can be implemented by anyone who dares.

Introduction

Perhaps you have heard about the Alpha management style — the one based on the masculine, authoritative use of power.

Perhaps you have also heard about the Beta management style — the one based on the feminine, cooperative use of power.

In this book I will introduce what I call the Omega management style — the style that incorporates and enhances them both.

Jesus, CEO: Using Ancient Wisdom for Visionary Leadership is based on three simple premises:

1. One person trained twelve human beings who went on to so influence the world that time itself is now recorded as being before (B.C.) or after (A.D.) his existence.

2. This person worked with a staff that was totally human and not divine . . . a staff that in spite of illiteracy, questionable backgrounds, fractious feelings, and momentary cowardice went on to accomplish the tasks he trained them to do. They did this for one main reason — to be with him again.

3. His leadership style was intended to be put to use by any of us.

The idea of Jesus as a Chief Executive Officer (CEO) came to me twenty years ago when I was living in the mountains. It struck me at the time that Jesus had many feminine values in management and that his approach with his staff often ran counter to other management styles and techniques I had both witnessed and experienced. As I started my own advertising agency ten years later and began to encounter businesses on many different levels, I was dismayed to find countless "homeless" people in corporations. I too often saw invaluable human energy and intelligence untapped and underutilized. I saw multiple examples of corporate abuse, neglect, and violence. I decided to write this book to help turn the tide and to empower people in all layers of leadership to re-*view* the divine excellence in themselves and in those they serve.

I also found it disturbing that nearly all leadership and management books are written by men. Yet women are the fastest-growing segment of business owners in this country. *USA Today* recently reported that soon women will employ more people than all the Fortune 500 companies combined. Similarly, nearly 80 percent of all businesses in the United States employ twenty people or less. Clearly, small groups of people led by innovative leaders and managers make up the strength, and hope, of this nation. With the business world changing so rapidly and so drastically, it seemed to me that we need creative and innovative role models now more than ever before. I believe the world is crying out for leaders whose goals are to build up, not to tear down; to nurture, not to exploit; to undergird and enhance, rather than to dominate. Jesus as a leader struck me as the noblest of them all.

I believe Jesus' "Omega" management style incorporates and transcends the best of the Alpha (masculine) and Beta (feminine) leadership styles, because by harnessing spiritual energy, each of us, female and male, can become the empowered leaders that the next millennium will require.

To those who are looking for tips on how to make a fast buck or get a quick management fix, this book will have little or no relevance. I am searching for people who are willing to plant the fields that lead to the harvest and who recognize that the workplace, where most of us spend the greater part of our lives, is indeed very holy and fertile ground.

The Selection Process

In your humanness, you might hope your new staff will have the powers of angels, but the first one pointed out to you smells not like heavenly phosphorescence but like mud and dead fish.

The next one is not drawn from the halls of a university but is out collecting taxes in the name of the government that everyone hates. The selection process continues. . . . Your staff and followers are plucked from trees, back alleys, and down at the pier.[1]

And as you gaze on your chosen few, you realize that this group will outlive you and must carry out the task you cannot accomplish without them: to change the world. You have three years to train them. What do you do?

This is the question that faced Jesus, a young leader . . . a leader who, like many of us, had to depend on others to accomplish a goal.

In studying Jesus' leadership techniques, I began to realize that he, the original Omega leader, had three categories of strengths:

- the strength of self-mastery
- the strength of action
- the strength of relationships

Currently you may be strong in only one or two of these areas. Yet success in management requires the total combination. For example, a physician who has self-mastery and action skills, but lacks relationship skills, will be limited in her/his career. Likewise, we are all too familiar with the downfall of political leaders who had relationship and action skills, but lacked strength in the area of self-mastery. The goal of this book is to heighten your awareness level in each category and to assist you in the process of mastering them all.

STRENGTH OF
SELF-MASTERY

Above all else, keep

watch over your heart,

for herein lie the

wellsprings of life.

PROVERBS 4:23

He said
"I Am"

What if Jesus did not instantly know who he was? Or what his gifts were? What if it dawned on him only gradually, as it dawns on each of us? Maybe his mother recited stories of the unusual events surrounding his birth. Maybe she set the beautiful boxes the three wise men brought him on a shelf in his room, and at night the young boy would take them down and hold them and wonder.

Or perhaps he knew instantly that he had a special calling and was just awaiting the moment when his powers could be set free. Either way, I believe Jesus had to go into the wilderness to find out who he was — that a wilderness experience was as much a part of his shaping and destiny as it is of yours and mine.

I was once involved in a meeting of real estate developers who were gathered to discuss a possible joint venture. Each developer had an impressive résumé in terms of the task to be accomplished. Much to our surprise, the organizer of the group stood and began to describe in detail one of his greatest failures. He talked about how his eagerness to make money for his investors had caused him to overlook some important details about public opinion trends. He said, "I am much more careful now to get all the facts before acting on my ideas." The person next to him then, with a slightly red face, admitted that on occasion he had not exactly been a genius, either. In fact, he once purchased a huge parcel of land for development that was, unbeknownst to him, sitting on solid rock.

The youngest member of the group was reluctant to speak when it was his turn to share his mistake. He sort of fumbled around and said, "Well, everyone knows I've had many successes." The leader gently chided him, "Come on, Charlie. Put your *rock* out on the table. If you have not experienced failure, you cannot be a part of this group."

What the leader was really saying was "If you have not been tested by fire, you do not know who you are.

And if you do not know who you are, you cannot be a leader."

In the wilderness, Jesus was given clear choices, each relating to his special gifts. When the Devil said, "Worship me and you will own the world," Jesus said, "No." The Devil said, "Then satisfy your hunger, and turn these stones into bread." Again, Jesus said, "No."

"Throw yourself off the pinnacle of the temple and test your power to spring back to eternal life." Jesus looked Satan in the face and said, "No." And finally, after forty days of being tested and refined in that desert furnace, a person emerged who was very clear about who he was and what he was called to do.[2] Jesus met the temptation to use his gifts selfishly, and he overcame them.

It is no coincidence that only after the wilderness experience did Jesus begin to use the words "I am" when describing himself.[3]

In the Old Testament, when the Jews asked God for a self-description, the only answer they received was "I AM that I AM."[4] The simplicity of this phrase emphasized his power to them. The words *I AM* therefore reflect all the creative power in the Universe.

Question

What wilderness experience has helped you see your gifts more clearly?

Q u e s t i o n

List in detail each of your own "I ams."

Q u e s t i o n

Write down three positive and powerful word pictures about yourself. Draw them. For example: "I am a bridge."

His "I Am"
Statements Are
What He Became

ᘛᘚ

Jesus did not look back on the events of his life and say, "Hmmm . . . I must have been the Son of God." He declared himself to be the Son of God,[5] and the proof followed.

Jesus regularly visualized the success of his efforts. "I declare a thing and it is done for me. My word accomplishes that which I send it out to do."[6]

Probably many people would describe Jesus as one of the most humble beings who ever walked the earth. Yet consider what he said about himself in the Bible. Absolutely everything he said about himself was positive.

"I always do what pleases God."[7] "God always answers my prayers."[8] Was this conceit? Or was it enlightened creativity and self-knowledge? If you look at the Old Testament, you will read some of its most beautiful verses recited later by Jesus about himself. For example, his mission statement regarding bringing good news to others is taken from the prophet Isaiah. He internalized beauty and claimed it as his own.

There is a proverb that says "A man's curses will fall and wrap themselves around him like a cloak." What a powerful visual image that is. What if every word we said fell and wrapped itself around us like a garment? What kind of wardrobe would we have?

Words have power. And Jesus always spoke loving, powerful, and confident words about himself.

It is interesting to listen to the self-talk of super-athletes. I once read an article in which one of the greatest female tennis players of all time reviewed a game that she lost. Every statement she made about herself was still positive. People who succeed speak well of themselves to themselves. Nowhere in the Gospel does Jesus put himself down. Jesus was full of self-knowledge and self-love.

His "I am" statements were what he became.

Question

Whom do you tell yourself that you are on a daily basis?

Question

If each word you said about yourself fell and wrapped itself around you like a garment, what would your self-talk "wardrobe" look like?

Question

What good, pure, true, and beautiful words do you feed your mind every day?

He Kept
in Constant
Contact with His Boss

ᘛᘚ

Each of us must answer to someone. Any sixth grader familiar with the food chain will tell you that even the king of the jungle ultimately becomes food for little insects. None of us is without someone who could ultimately "eat us for dinner." In fact, when a person begins to think there is no one to answer to, problems really begin.

Jesus knew who his boss was, and he kept in touch with him daily.

Ed Koch, one of the most reelected mayors of New York City, used to go around town asking the people he met "How am I doing?" The folks loved him for it, and many considered his openness to be one of the keys to his popularity.

Al Neuharth, founder of *USA Today* newspaper, drove around the country asking people what kind of newspaper they'd like to read. This man, earning over a million dollars a year in salary, considered his bosses to be the people who plunked the quarters into the newspaper vending machines. He took the time to stay in touch with the people he served.

An example of the consequences of not staying in touch occurred when the board of trustees for a national medical association decided to celebrate the organization's anniversary. They asked all members to donate 30 percent of their time to an anniversary gala. More than one state director told representatives from the national office (where this plan was hatched) that this plan was extremely unpopular with the state offices. The representatives, who often were hired just for their ability to say yes to the executive director, never mentioned the unpopularity of the plan to the board, as it was the director's pet project. When one newcomer attempted to bring it up at a board meeting, the director threw her such a look that she promptly shut up.

The board held its great kickoff celebration, to which the national media and key government cabinet members were invited; but only eleven people showed up. Nine were board members. Group members had spent nearly

$60,000 to promote their event but failed to purchase a two-cent cotton swab to clean out their ears before they launched it. The board members forgot to communicate with their boss(es), who were the members of the association they were representing. They ruled by mirrors, not by windows.

Jesus met with his boss daily, usually for hours. Nothing could interrupt the time that was predesignated, set aside, and honored.

As a leader, it is vitally important that you keep in touch with your boss on a regular, sacrosanct basis. Chances are your boss can provide an aerial view that will make your path more clear.

Jesus kept in constant contact with his boss.

Question

Do you know who your boss really is?

Question

Draw a picture of your "food chain."

Question

How regularly do you communicate with your boss?

He Stuck
to His Mission

～❦～

Jesus knew his mission statement, and he did not deviate from it. He declared that his mission was, in essence, to teach people about a better way of life. He saw himself as a teacher and a healer.

An ancient adage says "If you want to defeat them, distract them." In the wilderness Jesus was given several "business opportunities" that did not relate to his mission.

Each of these opportunities was related to talents that Jesus had, and used, in some form or another during his tenure. But he resisted them because they did not fit his mission statement.

Pause for a moment and consider the things Jesus

did not do. Here is someone endowed with limitless power from on high. He could have done literally anything. Yet he did not build a temple or a synagogue. He did not write or distribute books. He did not even heal all the sick people in the world. He did not go down to the graveyards and raise everyone from the dead. He did not build shopping malls. His mission was very specific.

Jesus stuck to his mission.

Question

What is your mission? Can you define it in one or two sentences?

Question

Do feelings stir inside you that suggest you might contribute to a better way of life for others?

Question

Can you list opportunities currently in your path that might really be distractions? What are they?

He Believed
in Himself

esus was one of the most confident beings who ever lived. He envisioned himself as a vital opening for the people. He called himself *The Gate* . . . *The Door*. He believed his role was also to nurture others. He called himself *The Vine* . . . *The Shepherd*. He said he came to light the way. In other words, he believed in himself down to his very toes.

Belief in oneself is a crucial quality of leadership, because "a house divided against itself cannot stand." A leader who fluctuates back and forth sends a very wavery signal. Like the soprano who can shatter glass by finding that high note and holding it, a leader who can hold that high note, without wavering, can shatter walls. Jesus had no ambivalence about who he was or what he was supposed to do.

I once attended a seminar where the leader asked, "How many of you believe in yourself 100 percent?" Two people raised their hands. As the leader went down the percentage scale, more and more people raised their hands. The majority of the people in the room believed in themselves 75 percent of the time. The leader then asked, "Why are you afraid to go that extra 25 percent? What do you think would happen?"

The group leader asked, "Do you realize that power is assumed, not granted?" I questioned this at first, but then I thought about the times when someone in a group setting took it over, whether he or she had the authority to do so or not. How do people get tapped for leadership positions even when they are not looking for them? Probably because they emanate self-confidence. They have power over themselves, and people pick up on that energy.

Perhaps we think 100 percent belief equals arrogance. Arrogance, however, is lack of self-confidence, not self-belief. Jesus was never arrogant or cocky to anyone. Even when he was bound and thrown before the Sanhedrin for trial, he was not arrogant. Nor did he deny his own power.

My father, an action-oriented person, was never known for his love of poetry. However, I'll never forget the day he sat down with me to plan my college career.

He said, "Laurie, I learned only one poem in school that stuck with me. Here it is: 'I bargained with life for a penny, only to learn, dismayed, that any wage I would have asked of life, life would have paid.'" He looked me straight in the eye and said, "Go for what you want. You can do anything you set your mind to."

What do you think the world would be like if people believed in themselves 100 percent? How much damage is done in this country and in the world every day because of humanity's low self-esteem?

How many times have people said:

"I don't think I have any real power, so I'm going to get a gun and show that guy who's really the boss."

"I can't really change my life, so I'd better escape it. Give me a drug."

"I'll never amount to much, so I might as well drown my sorrows. Make it a double."

"I'm afraid that you'll take my power away, so here's a fist, a knife, or a knuckle sandwich."

The list goes on and on. If only we believed in ourselves, the world would be a better place.

Jesus said he came from heaven and was going back to heaven. He came to teach us what heaven was like and how to bring it about on earth and, more important, in ourselves.

Jesus believed in himself 100 percent.

Question

How much do you believe in yourself?

Question

What would it take for you to believe in yourself down to your very toes?

He Had
Internal Anchors

Jesus said, "Why do you seek after people's approval but do not seek the approval that comes from only God?"[9] He was an effective leader because he had internal anchors. He did not get his approval from external mechanisms. His actions were not based on what Peter, John, and James thought. He didn't come unglued when John the Baptist began to doubt him. He didn't care whether Caesar smiled or frowned.

Have you ever experienced that euphoric bubble when you finally reach a decision that you know is right? People have various names for it — feeling centered, being right on, being in a state of grace. Those who have experienced this feeling say there is nothing to compare to it. One woman said it was like being out at sea and hearing only silence, even though she could see people waving their arms on the shore. Here is how she described it: "Nothing mattered as much to me as that still, silent point of being. Everything else seemed meaningless . . . almost like it was just a puppet show." She said she had never felt closer to God, even though the decision she made upset many people around her.

The Omega leader has a backbone like a rod of steel when it comes to doing the right thing. You may have to search for it, but once you hit the harmonic "C" — the note that matches perfectly with your soul — you, God, and destiny will be one *harmonious* sound. And others will stop, perk up their ears, and begin to gather around.

Jesus had internal anchors.

Question
What are your internal anchors?

Question
From whom do you seek approval?

He Guarded
His Energy

If you had the power to do anything, how would you decide what to do? This may seem like a minor problem, but look, for instance, at people who inherit large amounts of money. Many of them manage to make it disappear rather quickly. Likewise, people who have unlimited free time often find themselves involved in activities that ruin their health or peace of mind. Having too much can sometimes be as much of a burden as having too little.

Jesus had tremendous energy, and he knew how to direct it. He was so clear about his mission that he avoided many real and potential *energy leaks*. For example, even though he was a teacher, he refused to engage in meaningless debates with people who wanted not to learn but to argue. Even at his trial, he did not waste time or energy in what he knew would be a meaningless defense.

Although he was a recruiter of sorts, he never wasted energy begging or manipulating others to follow him. In fact, he trained his staff to "wipe the dust from their feet"[10] and to keep moving if people were resistant to his ideas. He also said not to "cast your pearls before swine,"[11] a very graphic image about the importance of knowing where and with whom to share the treasure of your energy.

Jesus was so aware of his energy that once when a woman reached out and grabbed his clothes in the middle of a crowd, he turned around and asked, "Who touched me?"[12] The staff members were astonished, since he was being pushed and shoved and crowded by many as they walked along. "Everybody's touching you," they said. "No, I felt power go out from me," he said. He then turned to face the woman, who asked to be healed. Her intense desire drew on his energy so that he could literally *feel* her faith.

We are told that he came through walls without opening doors, and of course he emerged from a sealed tomb. This man was a master of the physics of energy — especially his own — and he was very careful about how he used it.

How many *energy leaks* do we have in our own daily

lives? Leaks such as angry words, distractions, or tampering in someone else's business while neglecting our own.

To be a leader requires a tremendous amount of energy. Perhaps that is one reason why entertainers and rock stars often succumb to the energy boosts offered by alcohol or drugs. They are pouring out so much energy to the crowds that their own reserves get depleted. They then look for instant energy.

A close friend of mine who is known for her highly polished intuitive ability recently returned from a meeting where there had been many hidden agendas and open conflicts. She sat down with a heavy sigh and said wearily, "I think my psychic feelers have been damaged." She has learned to develop ways to replenish her "antennae." Quiet prayer, rest, and time alone are ways that work for her . . . as well as a good round of golf.

Most leaders are intuitive, or they would not be able to hear and see things that no one else can see or hear. Leaders must therefore be aware that their energy is subject to depletion, and they must make guarding that energy reserve a priority.

Energy is everywhere, but stillness plays a major role in its conversion from "potential" to "actualized" energy. At Callaway Gardens I was amazed to learn that butterflies *have* to spread their wings in the morning sunshine because the scales on their wings are actually solar cells. Without that source of energy, they cannot fly. It is no coincidence that most of the leaders and prophets in the Old Testament were shepherds — people with plenty of time to listen. If there is no snow in the mountains, there will be a drought in the plains. Everyone needs to be in tune with her or his source of energy.

Jesus guarded his energy.

Question

What daily *energy leaks* keep you from being focused?

Question

How do you replenish your energy reserve? How often?

He Did the
Difficult Things

One definition of a *professional* is a person who does things even when she or he does not feel like doing them. In other words, a professional is not blown about by the winds of the moment. Professionals stay focused on the successful accomplishment of their mission, and do the difficult things.

Many charismatic and popular leaders get into trouble when they cease doing the *difficult things* in order to win approval or be liked. Politicians who depend on opinion polls to determine their actions do not last very long as leaders. Unfortunately, if you run your management program based on opinion polls or popularity contests, you will not last long as a leader, either. "The tendency of the masses is towards mediocrity," said Aldous Huxley, and opinion polls are a very poor source of vision. Failing to do the difficult thing eventually will get you in trouble.

A once-popular televangelist had charisma, a clearly popular product or service, and a tremendous following. However, because he failed to assess and recognize fiscal priorities and responsibilities, he wound up in jail.

Maintaining that connection with your own inner knowing is so important. Doing the difficult thing means not letting public opinion sway you from what your heart, gut, spirit, or instinct is telling you.

Peter tried to stop Jesus from going to Jerusalem. He sensed danger there, and he was right. However, Jesus knew it was part of a larger plan. So, he "set his face towards Jerusalem,"[13] even knowing the consequences.

Perhaps the true mark of a leader is that she or he is willing to stand alone. It must have been difficult for Jesus to say no to people. The whole essence of his being seemed to say yes. But he did say no. He said no to the ambitious young man who wanted to follow him. He said no to his mother when she was trying to interrupt his teaching. He said no to Judas about turning to politics. He said no to temptations in the wilderness. He said no, at times, to himself: "No, I will not run from this. I will drink the cup that is placed before me."[14]

Leaders must have not only vision and communica-

STRENGTH OF SELF-MASTERY

tion skills but also tremendous personal resolve. While leaders attract followers, at any moment they must be able to walk away from them, lest they become followers themselves.

Jesus did the difficult things.

Question

What difficult things are your instincts, right now, telling you to do?

Question

Are you willing to do them, even if it means standing alone?

He Said
Thank You

Just before Jesus commanded Lazarus to rise, he
thanked God for always hearing him.[15] In one of his
final prayers, he thanked God for giving him Peter, John,
James, Mary, Martha, and the rest of his staff.[16] Jesus
had a thankful heart.

Gratitude is a key element of leadership because gratitude means an open heart, a listening heart, a faith-filled
heart. How could anyone be a leader without faith and
gratitude in a Higher Power or have a better future built
on better ways?

One of the most breathtaking sights in San Diego is
sunset on the beach. As the sun sinks slowly into the

horizon, hundreds of seagulls stand and turn quietly to bid farewell. Pelicans fly by in perfect formation, skimming just the top of the waves in their sunset salute. On the bridge across from the beach, thousands of birds line up on the electrical wires, all sitting and facing the sun, saying good-bye to the day. Perhaps they are also silently praying "Thank you, God, for knowing and caring when even one of us falls. Thank you, God, for declaring that even the sparrows shall be fed."

Jesus said thank you.

Question

Do you say thank you *before* you ask for something—from God, from your boss, from your staff?

Question

Do you realize that having a grateful heart may keep you from needing a transplanted one?

He Was
Constantly in a
State of Celebration

Perhaps Jesus loved celebrations so much because he was born at a party. I believe any event that has a heavenly light show, people bearing gifts from distant places, and a host of angels singing and giving directions is a celebration of major proportions. It must have made an impact on him.

One of his first miracles was to turn water into wine (not vinegar). As his fame and popularity grew, he was constantly invited to dinner at Nicodemus's or Peter's or rich young people's houses. The night before he was arrested, he gathered his staff together to sing songs and dine.

When crowds came, Jesus was adamant that nobody leave with an empty stomach. He always managed to locate food for them. He turned one boy's lunch into food for thousands.[17] He told stories of a king who arranged a banquet and then got angry and disappointed when nobody came. He spoke of a father throwing a lavish party to celebrate a wayward son's return. When Jesus returned from the dead, he prepared a fish barbecue on the shore — sort of a "team picnic."

He came from a very happy place, and he knew he was returning to a very happy place. When he said, "Wherever two or more are gathered in my name, there am I in the midst of them,"[18] perhaps he saw a party coming on. Indeed, his invitations read "I go to prepare a place [setting] for you."[19]

I think he is telling us to lighten up. "Why do you worry so?" he would ask. "Don't you see the flowers . . . how beautiful they are? Do you think your Father is going to let you wear less than these?"[20]

Once on one of my journeys I met a young man who, after we were introduced, said, "This calls for a celebration." He promptly went to the trunk of his Mercedes and pulled out a bottle of champagne. He was a very pleasant, clean-cut, and successful salesman with a contagious laugh and a great sense of fun. I asked him, "Do you always carry chilled champagne in the trunk of your car?" "Oh, yes," he said, lifting his glass to toast the occasion. "Life is full of opportunities to celebrate, and I don't want to miss any of them."

A ten-year-old once asked me if I knew what Jesus' first words were after he came out of the tomb. "No," I replied. "What were they?" He spread his arms, jumped forward with a grin, and said, "Ta-dah!"

Jesus was constantly in a state of celebration.

Question

How often . . . and what . . . do you celebrate?

Question

Do you celebrate only the big things? What are some small things to celebrate?

Question

When was your last celebration?

He Owned It

Ownership is an interesting and elusive concept because it implies a permanent state of possession. Yet all things, even life itself, are only on loan to us. Author and management consultant Ken Blanchard says that visionary leaders are those who view life's resources as being on loan to them, while more limited thinkers are still in an "acquisition" mode.

One year for my birthday an artist friend of mine, declaring that he had a surprise for me, took me blindfolded up a long winding road at sunset, stopped the car at an especially scenic point, removed the blindfold, and had me slowly open my eyes. There before me was the city coming alive with little twinkling lights . . . as if God had scattered iridescent diamonds across a black velvet sea. "For your birthday I give you this," he said. "The entire city is yours."

I wonder if God whispered these same words to Jesus as he sent him into the world. Jesus clearly demonstrated a sense of ownership of all things. Whether the need was a donkey to carry him into town, an upper room to pray in, wine for a wedding, or even coins to pay Caesar's tax, Jesus did not consider himself a beggar king. He used his divine sense of ownership to create the goods he needed when he needed them. And many times what he needed was delivered through the generosity and willingness of those he served.

Jesus' sense of ownership did not give him a sense of noblesse oblige, however. The joke is told about a famous writer whose friend finally told him he was no longer welcome at his home. "Why not?" the writer demanded through a bleary-eyed hangover. "Well, Ernest, frankly it's because you come into town, eat all my food, drink all my wine, and run the help ragged with your demands. And besides all that, I really don't like the way you've been looking at my wife." "Well," said the writer in surprise and disgust. "Then what are friends for?"

In the Garden of Eden God told Adam and Eve, "I

give you all this. Take care of it."[21] He told Abraham the same thing: "All of this land is yours."[22] Jesus described himself in one parable as the "Husbandman" who had been sent to take care of the vineyard. He looked at the world and the people in it as his responsibility, his inheritance, and his heritage. The whole universe was his and he knew it. Perhaps that is one reason why the people called him "King." It was the way he looked at the world and carried himself in it.

Jesus said, "All that the Father has is mine." Every galaxy, every newborn sheep, every fish leaping into the net, all that the Father had was his, and he knew it. He "owned it."

If only each of us could get a good look at the heavenly "deed" written in our name. If only we could study it and know our inheritance by heart, we would walk on this planet a different way. With more gentleness, perhaps, and more certainty and power. In order to own a gift you must first receive it.

Jesus had power because he "owned" it.

Question
What do you really *own*, with a deep-down-in-your-heart knowing?

Question

What are you trying to *own?*

Question

How can you truly *own* it?

He Did Not
Waste His Time
Judging Others

Jesus saw judging others as a major *energy leak*. He stated many times that he did not come to judge but that he came to help. He did not spend one minute on the demolition crew. He spent his energy on creation and restoration. Judging others was not his job.

He said, "I do not judge you. Your own words judge you."[23] He knew our accountability. He trusted each of us with our choices.

Judgment halts progress. When we as leaders judge others, we inhibit our own forward motion. Also, when we judge others, we are not doing our job because we are not in sync with the energy that moves *us* forward.

Sometimes we judge others in ways we are unaware of, such as looking to see where they are in the race.

Jesus said to Peter, "What business is it of yours what I say to John?"[24] Keep your eyes on your own forward motion.

He judged no one because he knew the final count was not in yet. Even the thief nailed on the cross beside him made it into Paradise because, with his dying breath, he acknowledged and saw the truth. Jesus said, "C'mon, buddy. We're going home. I want you to meet my dad."[25]

Jesus did not waste his time or energy judging others.

Question

Do you have energy leaks caused by judging others?

Question

What kinds of things can you do to support instead of judge?

He Expressed Himself

Many of the most highly paid people in our country are entertainers, actors, and athletes. What do they have in common, and why do we honor them so much with our discretionary dollars? I believe we pay these people to express themselves on our behalf.

We are inspired when actors dance with wolves. We are thrilled when actresses solve mysteries. We jump for joy when athletes fly into the air and slam dunk the ball. We love it when these people express our dreams, our hopes, and our fantasies.

I think we are a very repressed society, and because so many of us cannot seem to find our own expressions, we idolize those who can and do. When Elvis was on stage rocking and rolling, he was saying "Man, sometimes the music just takes me over." The people in the audience swooned because they wanted the music to overtake them, too. Elvis gave them permission.

When tennis players like Gabriela Sabatini and Steffi Graf hammer a tennis ball across the court, we feel like we are out there sweating, too. We can feel the power surge in our muscles and veins.

When Clark Gable sweeps Scarlett off her feet or when magician David Copperfield makes tigers disappear on stage, we are quickly swept up in the fantasy. We watch in awe and wonder, and we eagerly pay to do so. These people are very talented, and in many ways they are the outlets we choose for our own self-expression.

A close friend of mine is a probation officer who works with gang members in juvenile prison. These are kids who drive by and shoot strangers on the streets. She is developing a program to help them learn to express themselves better. "They seem to know only two emotions," she says. "Rage and loyalty. I am trying to teach them that there is a whole spectrum of emotions they can experience, not just red or black." Her big breakthrough came with a young man named Jimmy who was always mouthing off about how angry he was. "Are you angry or just disappointed?" she asked. "Look at the feeling chart and be specific." He thought a long moment and then slowly pointed to the word *disappointed*. Perhaps being unable to accurately express and identify raw emotions is a major cause of violence.

Our incredible God-given senses are of no value if we fry them and dull them with chemicals like alcohol and drugs. Orchestras of emotion are repressed when we just mumble "oh, well" or "never mind" and let moments for expression pass. If we keep painting over the graffiti left by gang members, (or staff workers), we will never take the time to figure out what they are trying to say. What good is it to paint over feelings, anyway? Ultimately they always will bleed through.

Jesus expressed himself aloud and often. He gave clear messages about how he felt regarding situations and people. He knew how to feel, and he voiced his feelings.

The Gospel of Mark includes a moving story about a young boy who had a spirit of deafness and dumbness that would "cause him to go rigid and try to throw himself in the fire." The boy's father came to Jesus and asked, "If you can help us, please do so." "If I can?" replied Jesus. "Everything is possible for one who has faith." Jesus rebuked the deaf and dumb spirit. And then Mark says, "Jesus took the boy by the hand and helped him up, and then he was able to stand."[26]

Reflect with me for a moment on this verse: "The spirit of deafness and dumbness was a spirit so painful it was causing the boy to throw himself on the fire." This sounds like the same spirit that plagues many of our young people today. Gang violence is on the rise. Teenage suicides are taking place in epidemic numbers. Perhaps our youth are throwing themselves on the fire because of society's inability to hear and help them express real feelings. Perhaps *our* spiritual deafness and dumbness is the demon that is wreaking havoc with our children's future and our own.

Jesus expressed himself, and he helped others to do the same.

Question

What feelings are you trying to numb with work, excessive activity, or synthetic substances?

Question

What do you use or buy to numb your feelings?

Question

Whom do you pay to express themselves on your behalf (for example, politicians, actors, writers)?

Question

What does it cost you to do that? Financially? Emotionally?

He Was Willing
to Look Foolish

~&~

What do each of these characters have in common?

- A deluded engineer
- A magician
- A waiter
- A nudist
- A beggar
- A lunatic
- A harem girl
- An improper woman
- A blasphemer

These were *roles* assumed or assigned to the following:

- Noah (designed and built the ark in the middle of a desert)
- Moses (turned water into blood)
- Nehemiah (was cupbearer to a king)
- Isaiah (went naked for three years)
- Elijah (had to ask a widow for food)
- King David (acted insane to escape his captors)
- Queen Esther (made her way to the top of the king's list)
- Mary (conceived a child before marriage)
- Jesus (claimed to be equal to God)

God has little use for people whose main concern is "What will the neighbors think?" Leaders must be willing to sacrifice and take risks with their public image.

Can you imagine a group of bankers sitting around a table when a young earnest man looks them in the eyes and says, "I am going to build a billion-dollar empire based on a mouse, a fairy, and seven dwarfs. Will you help me?" He would have been laughed out of the building. This earnest man, as you probably surmised, was Walt Disney. Now, however, the bulk of the current Disney team's activity consists of distributing and managing the ideas and characters created by this "silly cartoonist."

Ron Grover, in his book *The Disney Touch*, tells the

story of Roy Disney. Roy was Walt's more fiscally minded brother, who was always trying to put the brakes on Walt's "foolishness." After Disneyland was built, Roy lovingly told Walt that they did not need any more new ideas. In fact, Roy forbade Walt from spending any more money on the creation of new ideas.

With his own money, Walt formed a team of engineers who secretly met at night in a warehouse on the Disney lot. This crew developed the concept of EPCOT Center. Walt was a man who kept on thinking "foolishly."

Grover also relates how Michael Eisner, credited as half of the genius team that has guided Disney to its current economic status, was almost not hired. One of the major stockholders described him as a young man who "mostly liked to take the blocks he had and just rearrange them." To this, a higher-ranking member of the board replied, "This is exactly the kind of leader we need. Hire him and find ten more just like him."

Walt Disney went bankrupt in his first business endeavor. Thomas Edison had thousands of failures before he got the light bulb right. Benjamin Franklin, the fool on the roof flying a kite in a rainstorm, retired as one of our country's first millionaires.

Jesus was willing to look foolish. And this was the key to his success. Coming into town on a donkey, having to fish to pay your taxes, and forgetting to bring the wine do not seem like ingredients for success. Crying like a rejected lover, passing out invitations to a feast that largely go unanswered, having to stand on front porches and knock hardly sounds like a job description for a king.

Omega leaders cannot be afraid to look foolish. We must keep to the plan that we vaguely sense but that only God can see.

He was willing to look foolish.

Question

Are you willing to look foolish as a leader?

Question

List ten leaders who at one time or another looked foolish to the world.

He Did Not
Kick the Donkey

The Old Testament tells a story about the prophet Balaam. He was on a misguided mission to curse someone when his donkey suddenly stopped on the road. No
matter how hard the prophet kicked her, she would not
budge. Without the donkey, Balaam could not carry out
his deed. He proceeded to beat the donkey severely, apparently practicing the management style of ruling through
fear and intimidation. Finally the donkey cried out, "Why
are you beating me? Haven't I served you faithfully all
these years?" An angel spoke to Balaam and said, "You
fool, quit beating her. Even she could see I was standing
here. Your donkey just saved your life, for if you had

carried out this mission you would have been killed. In fact, I would have killed you and let the donkey live." The angel then left, and I can just imagine Balaam kissing the donkey all the way back to the stable.[27]

There is a fine line between knowing when opposition is God trying to show you another way or when it is just a test of courage. If the passively opposing forces cause you to use violence to get them to move, you probably are not on God's path. If you do everything you possibly can to get something to happen, and it doesn't, then an angel must be on the road somewhere, so don't beat the donkey. Take a little time out, smell the flowers, and re-think your route . . . and your mission.

When the Roman guards came to arrest Jesus, Peter sprang to his defense and prepared to engage in massive violence. He actually did cut off one guard's ear.[28] Here was a chance for Jesus to escape, but he knew that the Roman guard was part of the plan. He did not kick the Roman "donkey." He knew it was time.

Bernie Siegel, M.D., shocks his cancer patients when he asks them, "Why did you need this illness?" He claims that our bodies break down to give us a message . . . and many times it is a message that we have been ignoring. According to Dr. Siegel, while nobody wants to be ill, many patients say that cancer was the best thing that ever happened to them. They learned to appreciate life and to express their feelings to their loved ones. They were able to pick up the paintbrush they previously had been too busy to hold. Even illness can be a blessing.

Flat tires that keep us from catching a plane . . . missed appointments that cause a project's delay . . . bankers who tell us no . . . all of these can be donkeys that are keeping us from endangering ourselves in ways we cannot see.

Many times when you feel farthest from the truth, you are very close to it. And when you think you are on top of the world, you can be sitting in a very dangerous place.

When the donkey you are riding suddenly refuses to move, don't kick it. Get off and look for the angel standing in the road. That donkey might be saving your life. (They weren't given big ears for nothing.)

Jesus did not kick the donkey.

Question
Which circumstances in your life remind you most of the balking donkey?

Question
When has a "balking donkey" actually protected you?

He Had a Passionate
Commitment to the Cause

꿹

A friend of mine once asked, "What do you think Jesus was trying to teach his staff when he drove the money changers from the temple?"[29] I told him I thought he was reading too much into it.

Some say that he did it to show God's contempt for greed; others say that he simply lost his temper. I think his heart just filled with emotion that spilled over into action. Call it rage or righteousness, there was definitely strong emotion there. Leaders know how to shout and cry, and they often need to.

Tom Peters, the famed author, lecturer, and consultant, will often shout, yell, and stomp his feet when consulting with clients to protest some stupid or archaic policy. Some people think he can get away with that kind of behavior because he is already famous. I say that one of the reasons he became so famous was because he does not cover up his passion . . . he is totally committed to *excellence*.

A leader who is not passionately committed to the cause will not draw much commitment from others. The world will make way for someone who knows what he or she wants, because there is not much competition when it comes to passionate commitment. The Scriptures include examples of God's reaction to noncommitment. Jesus said, "It is better to be hot as fire or cold as ice, because if you are lukewarm I will spit you out."[30] He constantly warned his staff of the importance of commitment to his cause. He was willing to walk the road alone — and did — when it came to the price of his commitment.

One of my favorite examples of passionate commitment is the story of Elijah challenging the prophets of Baal and their idols. Elijah told the nonbelievers he would prove there was only one God by asking God to rain down fire from heaven to consume his sacrifice. Elijah said, "If God does not honor my prayer, then your gods are real and you can kill me." He cut up a sacrifice into many pieces and laid it out on the altar. He then poured water over it to eliminate any doubt as to the source of the fire. Then, surrounded by hordes of his potential executioners, he called out to the heavens, "Okay, God, prove what I said." Fire immediately came down and consumed the sacrifice right before their startled eyes. *That* was committed leadership.[31]

Elijah had *fire*. When Elijah was getting ready to leave the earth, he asked his protégé, the prophet Elisha, what he wanted. Elisha promptly asked for a double dose of Elijah's spirit.[32] He got it. Elisha received so much committed energy toward God that, years later, some soldiers threw a dead man on top of Elisha's grave and the dead man instantly sprang to life. Call it legend if you must, but the point of the power of influence is well made. Influence will outlast a person's physical lifetime when committed energy is there.

Sometimes passionate commitment to a cause is not so immediately obvious. I have often marveled at Georgia O'Keeffe's dedication to her art. She was so committed to her painting that she spent six months a year alone out in the desert where she could "better see the colors." Many criticized her for leaving her husband for such long periods of time. O'Keeffe was not famous for her sparkling wit at the dinner table, and she probably would not have won many popularity contests. In fact, she hated interruptions so much that in her later years, she hired a mute servant so that she would not have to talk and visit with him when he brought her breakfast.

This dedication to a craft may seem a bit extreme.

However, I stood in line for an hour and a half waiting to see her exhibition in Los Angeles, along with others who also had come to view the results of this woman's passionate commitment. I saw couples dropped off by limousines, dripping with jewelry and "Hello darlings." I also saw teenagers with green Mohawk haircuts and dog collars wrapped around their necks. There were Joe and Betty Everydays and a congregation of little kids from a local Baptist church. There were people on crutches, a woman with a respirator, and a young man in a wheelchair. The line to see Georgia O'Keeffe's art wrapped two times around the building. What would we have missed if Georgia O'Keeffe had not had a passionate commitment to her cause? What if she had spent her time succumbing to social demands, serving hors d'oeuvres instead of masterpieces?

Georgia O'Keeffe was a leader among artists around the world. She honored her commitment to the expression of beauty, no matter what the cost.

Nelson Mandela did not become a leader for black freedom merely because he was handsome or charismatic. He forged his influence across the world by marking time in jail cells and walking down lonely roads. For more than twenty years he sat in prison, refusing to compromise his commitment to freedom — because he believed it was not just an issue for himself, but for all people.

Jesus asked his staff members, "Can you really follow me?"[33] As it is with so many leaders, everyone wanted to sit next to him at the banquet, but nobody wanted to help him clean out the basement. Everyone was euphoric at the Palm Sunday celebration when they were laying palm leaves before his feet, but nobody wanted to walk with him when he made his final ascent up a hill that was so ugly and lonely its very name means "The Skull."

Leaders must be willing to walk up the hill alone. They must have a passionate commitment.

Jesus had a passionate commitment to the cause.

Question

Do you have a passionate commitment to a cause?

Question

How do you show your commitment?

He Requested
Noble Things

In thinking about the leaders in the Bible, I began to study their prayer requests. Many of them had opportunities when God said, "I will give you whatever you ask." How did these people cash in on the Heavenly Lotto? To my surprise, I noticed that all of them asked only for noble things.

> Abraham's request: "Help me follow you."
> Moses's request: "Help me free your people."
> David's request: "Help me slay the giant threatening our people."
> Esther: "Help me save these people."

Solomon: "Give me wisdom to rule your people."
Isaiah: "Give me clean lips to speak your words."
Peter: "Help me feed your sheep."
Jesus: "Help me show them Your love."

There is one verse that says "The noble person plans only noble things."[34]

Jesus was a leader who requested only noble things. He asked for healing, for forgiveness, for love. At the age of twelve he claimed the verses from Isaiah 61 as his mission: "He has sent me to bring good news to the poor, to bind up hearts that are broken, to proclaim liberty to the captives . . . to comfort all those who mourn, and to give them for ashes a garland . . . for a mourning robe the oil of gladness, for despondency, praise." Jesus asked for noble things.

"Noble" is such a beautiful word, but one doesn't hear it mentioned very much anymore. The *Wall Street Journal* never runs a story about "The Ten Most Noble Companies." *Inc.* magazine doesn't carry articles on "How to Be a Noble CEO." The book *Think and Grow Rich* by Napoleon Hill might not have sold so well if it had been titled *Think and Grow Noble*.

But I think people are basically noble at the core. When articles run in the paper about some tragedy that hits a poor family, donations pour in by the thousands. Recently on a *Good Morning America* segment, a financial analyst stated that although we pay billions in taxes in this country, we donate billions of dollars above that.

Why can't we have another Camelot—a group of people fully dedicated to nobility and its pursuits?

Tonight in my prayer requests, I'm going to think about noble things, such as how to shine more light in a world cursing the darkness . . . how to contribute more to the noble causes in the world. Maybe, if we each think about it more, we, like other leaders in the past, can become "nobility." Because we have asked for noble things.

Jesus asked for noble things.

Question
What noble things are you praying for?

Question
Who else is praying for and doing noble things?

Question
How can you help them?

He Saw Love
in Control
of the Plan

King David was a poet, an athlete, a dancer, a shepherd, a warrior, a singer, and a musician. He was passion personified.

One story about King David is particularly intriguing. When his popularity in the polls was very low, Shimei (a man from the family of Saul) began cursing him and throwing rocks at him. David's incensed and loyal army wanted to destroy Shimei immediately, but David said, "No. Who knows? Perhaps God has sent him to curse me."[35] This response is surprising because in the Psalms, David sometimes expressed desires for violent revenge. In this case, however, David did not display it. He also turned down three opportunities to kill Saul. He called him "God's anointed," even after Saul had obviously gone insane and was trying to kill him. When the opportunity came for David to easily destroy someone else who was making his life miserable, he said, "No, because perhaps he was sent from God."

When Pilate threw Jesus into prison, Jesus said, "You would have no authority over me if it were not given to you from on high."[36] In other words, he saw the soldiers and even the trial as being part of God's plan. Both David and Jesus were able mentally to accept and integrate injustice as being part of a larger, loving plan.

Bad things do happen to good people. For many, life is a struggle that seems unfair. Author and minister Terry Cole Whitaker told the following story from Dan Millman, which demonstrates that we cannot judge things as being good or bad because we do not have access to all the information.

One day a man bought a stallion, and all of his friends said, "That's good." The next day the stallion ran away, and all of his friends said, "That's bad." Two weeks later the stallion returned with a herd of mares. His friends said, "That's good." The next day his son broke his shoulder when the stallion threw him off. The friends said, "That's bad." The next month war broke out. Because the boy was injured, he could not go to war. The friends said, "That's good."

The story could go on and on with people judging events as being bad or good when actually all the events are connected and have an impact on each other. Trying to sort *good* from *bad* and putting labels on events that are constantly changing their shape can make a leader crazy. Yet David could endure the insults and Jesus was calm when his life and his work seemed to be unraveling before his very eyes. He had done everything he could. The rest was in higher, larger hands. He believed and knew that love was in control of the plan.

Paul said in Romans 8:28 that "all things work together for the good of those who are called according to God's purpose."

In Psalm 139 David says, "You knew me when I was in my mother's womb. You laid out all my days, when as yet there were none of them." In the midst of doubt and turmoil, he also wrote a beautiful song to his soul, which I repeat to myself when things seem to be going awry.

All in order, well assured,
does He not bring to flower
all that saves me,
all I desire?[37]

This too was Jesus' philosophy of life.

He saw God as his only source, and love in control of the plan.

Question

What *bad things* in your life right now could be turned into something good?

Question

List any good things that have resulted from a "bad" situation in the past.

Question

Whom do you tend to blame when big or little things go wrong?

Question

Whom did Jesus blame?

He Worked
Through His Fears

Jesus was afraid. He talked about his fears to his staff. He wrestled with his fears to the point of sweating blood in the garden. Without fear, Jesus could not have been an example to us. He would have been just another man.

Years ago when I worked in a day care center, a little girl looked up at my 5'10" frame and said, "Wow. You're really tall!" "Yes, I am," I said. "And someday when you're all grown up, you will be tall, too." She looked up at me solemnly and said, "I'm not afraid."

Jesus was not afraid to grow up, either, but he did

have to face some painful and gruesome events in his life. He felt fear.

Susan Jeffers, Ph.D., has written a wonderful book called *Feel the Fear . . . and Do It Anyway*. She tells us that we will probably always have to deal with fear. If we wait for our fears to disappear before we start, we will never even begin.

Proverbs mentions the foolish farmer who waits for a cloudless sky before he plants his field. There is almost always a cloud somewhere in the sky, and those who are trained to look will probably see more than one. Waiting for the perfect time is a great excuse and rationalization to stay stuck where you are.

Jesus knew that the best way to conquer fear was to face forward. He did not shrink from going to Jerusalem. He boldly announced his identity to his executioners. He got sick to his stomach and wept till sweat became blood — but he went through it. Although he felt fear, he faced it.

Fear is an ever-present fact of life. This point became clear to me a few years ago when I led a group of female physicians through an exercise in visualization. One woman volunteered to be the Heroine and to take a ring across the room and place it in a heavily guarded chalice. Two women volunteered to be the Heroine's worst Fears. The rule was that the Fears could not touch her, but they could do everything else in their power to keep her from putting that ring in the cup.

The Fears shouted and hooted and waved their arms and stood on top of chairs trying to block her view of the cup. They did all sorts of fearful things, but the Heroine just kept moving forward until she achieved her goal. The Fears were making noises and trying to distract her even as she dropped the ring in the chalice. They never left the room.

Jesus worked through his fears.

Question

What are the fears that are keeping you from your goals?

Question

Assuming that your fears will never disappear, how long are you willing to wait to move forward?

He Was
Keenly Aware
of His Resources

❧

Jesus had an astonishing ability to create what he needed from something that was already there. He took what was at hand and used his command of energy and universal principles — the same ones he said were available to us — and then created what he needed.

A Bible story that many of us might identify with is that of the staff member who tells Jesus that the group is in trouble because they have not paid their taxes yet. Jesus casually tells him to go down to the sea, and there he will find a fish with a coin in its mouth. "Use that to pay the tax," he said.[38]

Another time Jesus told his staff to go to a certain

location where they would find a donkey. He instructed them to tell the people that the master needed it and to bring the donkey to him.[39] Yet another time he made one loaf of bread feed thousands.

Perhaps part of Jesus' creative ability came from his deep understanding of the physics of faith and from his keen awareness of the resources that he did have. Jesus himself did not just appear in a cloud of cosmic dust. He came into this world through the body of a believing human being — Mary. God, too, is aware of his resources.

I often ask my clients to make a list of their resources, and I remind them that money is the least important one. It takes people some time to appreciate that their greatest resources are often the people they know. Joe Girard, in his book *The Greatest Salesman of All Time*, claims that he pictures the number 250 engraved on each person he meets. He says each person knows at least 250 other people he needs to know — people who could become his friends and customers, too.

It is important to take the time to know your people. Situations will come up where their many skills or talents or friends or relatives will prove invaluable. If you think of your pocketbook as your only resource, you constantly will be thumbing through the Yellow Pages instead of relying on someone you know.

A young physician started his practice, hoping to market his sports medicine skills. He spent thousands of dollars advertising in the newspaper week after week with very little result. One day as he was bemoaning his lack of business to his receptionist, she casually said, "My husband is president of the local jogging club. Why don't you do a seminar for them next week?" That was just what he was looking for: one human being, close at hand, with the resources he needed. Soon his practice was filled with people who knew someone whom he knew.

Jesus was keenly aware of his resources.

Question
How aware are you of all your resources?

Question
How many of your staff members' "250 contacts" do you know?

Question
How frequently do you update and review all the resources in your Rolodex?

He Felt a
Sense of Destiny

Do you sense you were destined to be doing what you are doing? If not, perhaps you have not yet found your *harmonic C*.

Jesus said, "I know where I came from and I know where I am going."[40] Although he may not have known every detail of his journey, Jesus felt a sense of destiny about his life. When the storm arose that threatened to sink his ship, he slept calmly, knowing it was not his time to die. Even when he was turned over to the authorities, he said to them, "You could have no power over me unless it was given to you from on high."[41] In other words, it had to be part of the plan.

The feeling of destiny involves a key element, which a friend recently shared with me. He said, "Great leaders inspire others to the extent that they inspire themselves." It took a moment before his words made sense. When you are surrounded by that state of grace where nothing else matters except the feeling you have within yourself, that is your intersection with destiny.

A woman I once knew had felt (and for a long time fought) the call to be a preacher. One day she recalled, "One thing kept me coming back." "What?" I asked her. "Well, whenever I would stand up and start talking about the Lord, my lips would tingle. It was as if my cells were dancing because they were doing what they were meant to do."

If our cells contain DNA molecules that determine what we are supposed to look like, isn't it possible that at some level they also know — and can recognize — what we are supposed to act like? People get emotional goose bumps when something strikes them as a moment of truth and destiny. As Paul said, "I will know, even as I am known."[42]

I believe that your destiny is like a magnet that pulls you — not a brass ring that only goes around once.

Jesus felt a sense of destiny.

Question

Do you feel as if you were destined to be doing what you are doing? Why or why not?

Question

What small voice might be calling you that you have been ignoring? What is it saying?

Question

What if the voice is right? What would change in your life—for the better?

Question

Do you believe any leader can lead effectively without feeling destined to do so?

Question

What if that still-small voice became a drumbeat, getting louder and louder? What would change in your life?

He Prized the Seed Rather than the Bouquet

Which would you rather have, a bouquet of flowers or a packet of seeds? Probably most of us would choose the bouquet. But if you are a leader, you realize the limitations of cut flowers, no matter how beautiful they are, and are more apt to spend your time gathering, sorting, and planting seeds.

Abraham Lincoln could have been showered with bouquets if he had acquiesced to the demands of the slave-owners; but he chose to plant the seeds of freedom for everyone and in so doing became a leader for all time.

Recently I had an interesting discussion with a businessman about Attila the Hun. In a speech I gave about assertiveness, I mentioned that using Attila the Hun as a role model for leadership was like studying Ted Bundy, the serial killer, and saying "Sure, he killed a lot of women, but let's look at how he got those dates!" The businessman, however, felt that Attila was a "success." In my opinion, he was not a success but a giant failure. He sowed the wind and reaped the whirlwind, being stabbed in the back by his newly "taken" bride. He raped and pillaged and plundered for a living. His whole leadership style was about ripping up flowers, not planting them, and this mentality is what has led our planet to the brink of ecological disaster.

During the recent recession, property values plunged in Southern California as well as around the country. When I decided to sell one of my "one too many" houses, I called the local real estate office and asked for the top-selling agent. I was given the name of Art Huskey, an agent who had just moved to San Diego from Yuma, Arizona, and yet had outsold every other agent that year. In fact, his sales were phenomenal. I signed with Art and quickly learned why his referral business is so incredibly high. He treats all his clients as if they were members of his own family.

He spent hours on the phone long distance with my mother, coaching her through an out-of-state real estate challenge, and never charged her. He referred friends of his to my mother when she relocated. These friends told Mom that Art sold them their first home years ago and in fact had actually "saved their lives." It seems the elderly couple had both come down with a severe form of flu. It was so debilitating that they could not even pick up a phone to ask for help. Art, after not hearing from them, went to their home and found them dangerously dehydrated. He took personal responsibility for them and even after they returned from the hospital brought them chicken soup for weeks. It seems every time I meet someone who knows Art, she or he has a similar story to tell.

Apparently, Art's true love is helping people, and real estate is just the venue that allows him to do that. In delivering chicken soup to them, was he just looking for another sale? Escrow had already closed. He had his check. But that didn't mean he stopped caring.

Unfortunately, with so many sales professionals, that commission check is just the bouquet they walk down the runway for, and then they are out the door. With Art, and people like him, that bouquet is the least of it. The true reward is sowing seeds.

I took a writing class one summer, and in it was a wonderful woman. She wrote a poem, which is reprinted here with her permission.

GARDENER
by Ann North

Some of the seeds of hope
Planted tentatively in the fall
Have not come up
They lie stillborn and unrealized
Somewhere in the spring soil
Decaying

The strongest and best ones
Pushed up through leaves
And layers of cold, hard resistance
Right into clear blue air
And stand there nakedly green
Breathing

It's always that way with growing things
Never knowing at the start
Which will make it and which will fail
But the thing to hold fast to
Never to lose faith in
Is simply
Sowing

Jesus could have ruled the earth. But his kingdom was not of this world. That is why he prized the seed more than the bouquet.

Question

What opportunities have you had recently to "take the bouquet" and run?

Question

How many seeds are in an apple?

Question

Which of your activities would change, and how, if you were more interested in the seeds you were planting than the bouquets you were receiving?

He Did Not Despise
the Little Things

In the Old Testament a verse reads, "A day of little things, no doubt, but who would dare despise it?" Jesus did not despise the little things. When he set out to change the world, he chose only a dozen people to work with — not a cast of thousands. He packed value into every minute, every glance, every question, every encounter because he knew that out of little things come big ones.

I see such an impatience with and disregard for little things in business that it disturbs me. Yesterday I listened to a woman lament that her bosses had taken away a key sale from an employee and "given" it to another one because it somehow made the store's overall cost of sales lower. Were they thinking that was just a minor incident to this salesperson? By trying to inflate the bottom line, they had punctured her trust and morale. "It was just a little sale," they assured her. Yet by depriving her of her little sale, they were losing their real customer — the employee herself.

I worked once with a boss who didn't want me to spend so much time with clients. "Go after the big clients, Laurie," he said. "Leave the peanuts to the others." And yet when the numbers were totaled, my combination of small sales outtotaled his few "big ones." I thought to myself (as I resigned to start my own company), "Dinosaurs became extinct — yet rabbits still abound."

Aren't many of us hounded by a sense that only the *big* things count? I personally have had to battle a mindset that said whatever I did had to be the biggest and the best. I couldn't just write a poem — it had to be *Ulysses*. Recently, out at Gold Rock Ranch, my artist friend Willy was teaching a group of us how to carve soapstone. Having seen her so quickly and easily carve out lovely shapes of bears and birds, I took my raw chunk of soapstone and began to study it intently. As if reading my mind, Willy called out, "All right, group, let's break for the afternoon while Laurie carves *The Last Supper*." I laughed and laughed. It was true. I thought surely I had to create — was about to create — a masterpiece on my first try. What I ended up with looked like a mix between a dove and a rocking chair — a silly little thing. Yet any creative person knows not to despise the little things — the first brush stroke, the first word on paper, the first phone call to a prospective client or friend. . . .

Jesus did not spend his time creating operations manuals that could be franchised and duplicated by the millions. He hurried to see a little girl who was sick, focusing only on getting her well; he knew that one boy's loaf of bread had all the ingredients necessary to feed thousands.

He did not despise the little things.

Question

How in your life or business are you "despising the day of little things"?

Question

What deed of yours today would you want to see multiplied?

STRENGTH
OF ACTION

She deploys her
strength from one
end of the earth to
the other, ordering
all things for good.

WISDOM 8 : 1
THE JERUSALEM BIBLE

He Saw
Everything
as Being Alive

O ne day Jesus was talking to the Pharisees, who were trying to determine how marriage contracts would work in heaven when one woman had married seven brothers, each of whom had died. (You can see why the Pharisees got so far in life, contemplating such issues. To me, the more significant question would have been what was it with this woman that all seven of her husbands died suddenly? I would have been checking her mustard sauce.) This question was of great concern to them, mostly because it was another opportunity to challenge Jesus' theology. Jesus turned to them and said, "People in heaven do not marry, for they are the same as the angels. But the larger issue here is that people do rise from the dead, and Moses himself said it. For you see, God is not a God of the dead, but of the living. For to him all people are in fact alive."[43]

"Lazarus, come forth!" he commanded. All things are alive. "Who is this man," the people marveled, "that even the wind and sea obey him?"

If all things are alive, then the road really may rise to greet you and the mountains may be persuaded to locate otherwise. "If you have faith, even the mountains shall obey you."

If one keeps Jesus' perspective that everything is alive, seemingly difficult things become so much easier. Walking through walls, for instance, becomes a matter of getting agreement from the cells of the wall. Walking on water simply becomes an exercise of the unity of cells. "Water cells, unite!"

Jesus saw everything — and everyone — as being alive and full of possibilities. Depression was simply energy yearning to be set free. Sinners were simply people who had not learned to sing in harmony. Jesus even knew that Calvary was a step back into another form of living.

Leaders should have more confidence, because everything is alive!

Jesus saw everything as being alive.

Question

What situations in your life have you written off as being "dead"?

Question

What opportunities have you written off?

Question

If you believed that everything was alive, how would your actions change—regarding work, your priorities, and the way you walk on the planet?

He Took
Action

❧

I have often wondered what God's drawing board must have looked like those first few days of creation. I have spent many silent moments walking through the aquarium at Scripps Institute of Oceanography contemplating the ethereal beauty of a jellyfish. The sea anemones wave their delicate tendrils, eager to reach out and touch someone. I gaze in wonder at the puffer fish and silvery brown sea bass that have a strange ultraviolet light hovering in their eyes. Several clown fish, which look like neon Popsicles, are also dancing in the tank. On the bottom, shrimp line up to clean parasites off other fish that swim slowly and methodically by. The Jacques Cousteau car wash, I suppose. The sea creatures remind me that God's imagination never quits.

In my study, I have a peacock feather dangling from a vase. The turquoise iridescence on each feather strand is a constant source of wonder to me. If you had created the peacock, wouldn't you have felt like quitting while you were ahead? But then you get the idea for a bird with a beak shaped like a banana and you start to draw again.

My biologist friend Cindy says that the only creature that has not grown or contributed to some other relative on the evolutionary scale is the sponge. She laughingly said at lunch one day that the sponge was either one of God's most perfect ideas or an artistic dead end, since nothing else developed along that line.

At any rate, create God did, and has, and does, and that power has not stopped creating. God is a thinking God, and as such must be coming up with new ideas constantly. Some people think that everything God created and said exists already. I do not think so.

I believe that is why Jesus came — to create new ways of thinking. To give us a *new* testament. He was not content to sit around and reminisce about what used to be. In fact, once he started teaching, he did not fail to create a word picture or two or three a day. John, the staff member who wrote about him in one of the four Gospels, said at the end of his story that if someone wrote down everything Jesus did, the world itself could not contain the books that would have to be written.[44] This was from someone who had known Jesus for only three years. Even in death, Jesus had his hands stretched out as far as they could go. People literally had to nail him down to keep him from doing more.

Jesus said, "My Father goes on working, and so do I."[45] He asked his staff to pray for more recruits because the fields were already bursting and ripe for harvest. Things needed to be done, and as a leader he wanted them done — even when he knew he would not be physically present to do them.

On the cross he looked down at John and said, "John, Mary is your mother now. And you must be her son."[46] By doing so, he was saying to all of us, "My work here is finished, but yours has just begun."

Jesus took action.

Question

How active and creative are you? Are you doing new things and stretching yourself, or are you just "being a sponge"?

Question

Do you think you could be doing more? If so, what? And how?

He Had
a Plan

A franchising consultant once told me, "A good idea is worth one dollar. The plan for implementing that idea is worth a million dollars."

A good leader has a plan. Jesus had one. He gave clear instructions to his staff members regarding how they could attain their desired results. He also had received a plan that he was working on implementing. He spoke often about how something was either part of or not part of the plan. He did not claim to know all the details, but he certainly saw the big picture and acted on a day-to-day basis according to his inner instructions.

What good does it do to stir up a crowd if you do

not give them a constructive outlet for their energy? So few people have plans that people will flock to almost anyone who comes up with a vivid sketch of how something should or could be done.

One of the soundest pieces of advice I received when starting my company was: Plan your work, and work your plan. When I wasn't feeling particularly bright or courageous, I just did what I had written on my list when I *was* feeling bright and courageous. Sometimes part of the plan was just showing up. In fact, more than one successful businessperson has confided to me that having a plan is the primary reason for their success. They show up when nobody else does, and they keep showing up. That is part of their plan.

A good leader has a plan that consists of changing simple pictures. Just because a group of people has a bunch of boards, hammers, and nails does not mean that they are building a house or even anything recognizable. Sometimes leaders think they are doing their job just because there is a lot of hammering going on. As a society we like the sound of hammering, but we are uncomfortable with the sound of thinking, which is silence.

Sometimes a plan can start with one simple objective. The civil rights movement was constructed around singular objectives. Sometimes they were as simple as: Make sure blacks do not have to sit in the back of the bus. *Equal rights* is an intangible idea. It is hard for people to grasp a concept that does not have pictures attached to it. Being forced to sit in the back of the bus creates a picture that people can get excited, angry, or motivated about. The desire to change that picture evolved into a plan.

Jesus had a plan.

Question
What is your plan?

Question
Is it written down?

Question
Is it clear?

Question
Can it be communicated?

Question
Is it workable?

Question
How can you implement it?

Question
When will you begin?

He Formed
a Team

Once Jesus began his work in earnest, he wasted no time in forming a team. It is as if he suddenly became magnetized. People were inexplicably drawn to him and he to them. "Follow me," he called out across the water, and without hesitation they followed. Even Jesus knew that he could not change the world alone.

I once had a discussion with a gentleman from another country who said he was envious of Americans' ability to form teams. "When your people want to get something done, they gather a group and assign the tasks. In my country, unfortunately, we do not have it so easy. Many of us cannot even seem to sit down together at the table. We spend years playing King of the Mountain, while your people have already figured out how to move it, save it, or make it bigger." One of the most important keys to successful teamwork is agreeing to agree.

If you as a leader or manager intend to accomplish anything significant, the first step toward attaining your goal is to create a team. Yet many people still feel they must do everything alone. We still have John Waynes and Super Moms who think it is wrong or a sign of weakness to ask for help.

Recently I met an engineer who developed a product that could help many people. He has not released it yet because he cannot come up with the perfect logo for his company. He feels that he has to do the logo, the brochure, the product development, and the marketing, too. No doubt he will paint his own building and grow his own corn, as well.

I am not mocking this man's individualism. I just wonder how far he can go with this particular belief system. The truth is that good ideas, noble intentions, brilliant inventions, and miraculous discoveries go nowhere unless somebody forms a team to act on them. Whoever forms a team to carry out the best ideas wins.

Jesus formed a team.

Question

What parts of a project are you still trying to do on your own? Why?

Question

Who is your real team, both paid and unpaid? Who could be?

Question

What challenge are you facing today? Who is facing it with you?

He Called
the Question

⟨꒰⟩

At board meetings, after countless discussions and motions, someone will usually say "Call the question, please," which means it is time to stop talking about the issue and take a vote. We love to discuss more than we like to decide. Jesus was constantly saying "Call the question, please."

A woman dreamed that she was being chased by a bear. When the bear finally cornered her, she asked in terror, "Are you going to kill me?" The bear calmly replied, "I don't know, lady. You tell me. This is your dream." This is a frustrating story for some because she was required to come up with the answer, rather than it being imposed upon her.

I once trained as a telephone prayer counselor for a rather progressive and upbeat church. During this training we were told to allow people about three minutes to tell their story, then we were to say "Okay, that brings us to the question: What do you want to have happen now?" It is amazing how people will suddenly fall silent when confronted with their own point of power. It is much easier to whine than to decide.

Jesus empowered people because he was willing to call the question "Who do you think I am? Who do you think you are? What do you want? Where is your heart?" He asked question after question. Perhaps he asked so many questions because one of his mottos was "You shall know the truth, and the truth shall make you free."

The truth is not always on the top shelf, front and center, either. Sometimes it is wrapped in yards of our delusions and is hidden in the basement. Two personal examples of this come to mind.

Many of us remember the story "The Emperor's New Clothes." Yet every day in the workplace we let people run around "naked" and pretend to admire the hat they are wearing. Wouldn't it be more loving to call the question? "John, I am sorry the report is not in. But is something else really bothering you? You have seemed awfully edgy lately. Is there anything you want to talk about?" or "Debbie, you haven't been smiling as much as usual. Is there something going on at home that is causing you to be unhappy?" Sometimes calling the question means taking the time to look into people's hearts.

An example of calling the question took place recently at one of the companies where I consult. Through untimely and unfortunate circumstances, a man was thrust into a new position for which he was not trained. He hated the job, but he did not want to say anything to rock the boat. The group that hired him (in an emotional response to his wife's death) was so sympathetic that they did not want to say anything, either. Tensions rose until finally one day at a board meeting, the newly elected president said, "Bill, you really don't want to be here, do you?" At first Bill obliquely defended himself from what he perceived to be a personal attack. As the discussion continued, however, the truth was uncovered. No, he did not like the job, but he felt they needed him. They in turn shared that they felt he was misplaced but did not want to hurt his feelings. Meanwhile, of course, the office had become a hotbed of resentment and innuendoes. One leader had the courage to say "Doesn't this look like a duck?" while everyone else had been acting as if this were indeed a rooster. They gave Bill a generous separation package while they searched for a bird of a different feather. The office morale immediately improved.

I am amazed at how often we honor each others'

illusions. Perhaps we are afraid of a Grand Unmasking: If one of us is forced to tell the truth, we will all be expected to reveal our true inner selves. Then where would we be? Free. At least, that is what Jesus believed. The truth will set us free.

Jesus called the question.

Question
What situation do you have in your office, company, or community that currently resembles a case of "The Emperor's New Clothes"?

Question
What obvious situation have you been afraid to bring to light? Could you picture the positive results that might occur when the truth is unbound?

He Saw Things
Differently

~ ⌘ ~

Jesus did not always perceive situations the way others did. For example, in both recorded stories of his raising people from the dead — the little girl and Lazarus — Jesus actively resisted using the word *dead*. "She is not dead. She's sleeping."[47] Finally, in order to communicate with the crowds, he acquiesced to their understanding of the word, but only as a frame of reference so that he could explain and demonstrate the other, more permanent side of things. He saw beyond the current perception.

Jesus said, "The first shall be last, and the last shall be first."[48] This was another belief of his that showed he saw things differently. "Whoever would be the greatest must become the least."

I once challenged a church where I served on the board of directors to give money away during the offering. The premise was, if the church truly believes the principle of multiplication, then give the people seed money, and ask them to multiply it and bring back the increase. It was an interesting experiment. Several of us on the board put up the seed money, which was distributed during the offering in small bills. The people were asked to take it, multiply it, and bring back the increase the following week. The result was triple the usual Sunday offering. The church accountant, however, had too fragile a heart condition to repeat the experiment. Surprisingly, many people refused to take the money, which may reflect how little we really are open to receive.

A university experiment was conducted where students were told to either ask for or give away dollar bills to passersby. At the conclusion of the experiment, the students had received more dollar bills than they could give away. People were suspicious of money freely offered.

Jesus was always seeing things differently. Sometimes we can see only the underside of the tapestry, with all its nubs and knots and mismatched threads. Jesus could see both sides of the tapestry, and he came to tell us how it would turn out.

The Omega leader sees things that could be and should be, and works to make them reality.

Jesus saw things differently.

Question
What do you see differently—something that could or should be changed?

Question
What steps are you willing to take to make the necessary changes happen?

He Broke
Ranks

Jesus did not follow the crowd. He led it. He did not report the news. He made it happen.

Mark McCormack, in his book *The 110% Solution*, states that he does not think people should read the paper in the morning. He believes they are just getting information that is available to everyone and are therefore formulating their plans based on common knowledge. McCormack says that leaders are responsible for having *uncommon* knowledge. He spends his morning meditating how best to serve the needs of the day. He reads the paper in the evening, after he has done everything he can think of to do something noteworthy for himself, his family, or his company.

In this country, negative information is free. Positive information you have to search for, or, better yet — create.

David had to break ranks to take on the giant Goliath because his brothers and fellow Israelites were back in their tents, trembling in fear. Finding this situation counter to all he believed about himself and his people, David volunteered to go forth to fight the giant.[49] Astonishingly, it was his brothers who tried to keep him from doing the right and courageous thing.

It was the same situation with Joseph. His jealous brothers threw him in a well because they were tired of listening to how he stood apart from them. Families have very strong "corporate cultures" of their own, and anyone who dares to be different is bound to encounter resistance. To Jesus, his family was not necessarily his mother and brothers, but anyone who did the will of God. In other words, his true family was anyone with similar goals, plans, and visions who was willing to act on them, no matter what the cost.

There are so many dysfunctional families and groups in our society today that a person must have uncommon courage to break free. Sometimes breaking free may require drastic measures and cause conflict. Churches can be dysfunctional. Companies can be dysfunctional. Governments can be dysfunctional. Laws can be dysfunctional. And a leader who is not willing to break ranks is not a leader at all, but merely a puppet set up to maintain the status quo.

The Pharisees were dysfunctional religious leaders whom Jesus felt so strongly about that he called them "whited sepulchres, broods of vipers," and other choice words. He had such strong words for them because they were supposed to help set people free, yet instead they enslaved people for their own selfish gain. Jesus knew he had to step out of that crowd in order to set people free.

He broke ranks.

Question

If you did what was really in your heart, with whom or what would you come into conflict?

Question

Describe the troops that you are currently marching with.

Question

What fear of conflict is keeping you from being a leader?

He Came
from Left Field

Jesus was not exactly what the people had in mind for a leader. Nathanael, a potential apostle, said, "Examine the Scriptures yourself and see. Can anything good come out of Nazareth?"[50] Jesus was neither a warrior nor royalty. He wasn't exactly handsome, either, according to some writings. He not only came from the wrong *side* of town, he came from the wrong *town*. The man nobody would have considered wore the crown. Nothing that the learned ones could decipher from their libraries called for a carpenter king. Once again, God played *surprise*.

Few people consider themselves perfectly qualified to lead. We are influenced by the media as to what everyone and everything should look like. We know what Miss America should look like, just as we know what senators and CEOs should look like. It is easy to disqualify ourselves as leaders based on external characteristics alone.

Yet we also live in times of great upheaval and surprise. Playwrights are becoming presidents, prisoners are becoming premiers, and women who used to serve coffee and tea now serve as prime ministers. Leaders are coming out of left field . . . with a fresh perspective.

Our passion may be enough to qualify us as leaders. One vivid example of this happened recently in a professional association for which I was a consultant. At a long-range planning meeting, I led a visualization exercise where members of the committee shared their images of what was holding the profession back. Judy, who had long been on the committee, saw the profession as a knight who had been knocked off his mount and was struggling in quicksand. After the retreat, several people, moved by her clarity and passion, asked her if she had ever considered running for president of the association. She replied that the idea had crossed her mind, but she had not given it serious consideration until now. Besides, the nominating committee had met months ago and the roster of candidates was already confirmed.

Judy's colleagues persisted, however, and discovered in the by-laws that she could be nominated from the floor.

At the membership meeting, she and her cadre of comrades boldly proclaimed her nomination. For the first time someone in the group asked that the candidates be required to give a speech. Judy presented her vision for the profession in a five-minute speech, while the long-standing and approved candidate mumbled and muttered around. Judy was elected by a two-to-one margin — the woman who had not been prequalified by committee but had been preselected by her own passion for the cause.

The call to leadership can come from many directions and in many ways. I believe that the Old Testament indicates three ways that we are called to leadership: the burning heart, the burning bush, and the burning house.

The *burning heart* is the kind of call that David had. He said, "I'll go fight the giant! It isn't right that our people should tremble in their tents at his insults."[51] The *burning bush* is the kind of call that Moses had. It is a surprise approach to getting someone's attention. As you recall, Moses was called to leadership by seeing a miraculous burning bush.[52]

The *burning house* is the kind of call to leadership that Queen Esther had. Esther, concealing her identity as a Jew, had become the honored and favorite wife of a king. The king got tipsy one night and allowed one of his devious advisors to declare that all Jews should be destroyed. Esther's uncle met her at the gates to tell her of the plan.

He told her that if she did not reveal herself as a Jew, she and the whole nation would be destroyed. Risking her life and certainly her social standing, she revealed her identity to the king, who in an embarrassed fury hanged the man who plotted the Jews' destruction. Esther became a legendary leader among the Jews. She became a leader when her house was burning down.[53]

Nearly every leader in the Scriptures had doubts at one time or another. They often felt underqualified, forsaken, or abandoned. Yet those who were called were given the strength to carry out their missions. Then as now.

Jesus was another one of God's surprises.

He came from left field.

Question

In what ways do you "come from left field" as a leader?

Question

Which type of call to leadership have you experienced:

- the burning heart?
- the burning bush?
- the burning house?

Question

How have you surprised yourself and others with your leadership?

He Branched Out

Jesus did not distribute his message just in his hometown. In fact, he left home rather quickly, recognizing that all too often a prophet is without honor in his own country.

He took his message and hit the road, going wherever there was fertile ground. He looked at the whole territory and saw it as a field ripe for harvest. He quickly began recruiting workers to help him with his task.

The importance of branching out is depicted in many beautiful stories and images in the Scriptures. Isaiah encouraged his people to "Widen the space of your tent, stretch out your hangings freely, lengthen your ropes, make your tent pegs firm, for you will burst out to the right and to the left."[54] God told Abraham, "I will give you every inch of the ground you tread upon, as far as your eyes can see."[55] David said, "Like a victor I shout and throw my sandal over Edom."[56] The entire Book of Joshua is about the tribes of Israel branching out into the Promised Land.

God does not seem to want leaders to "settle" for a little piece of land, spiritual or otherwise. The Divine constantly urges us to lift up our eyes and see all the possibilities on the horizon and to shake off the dust and ashes from our minds and feet and get going.

The word *branch* or *branches* is mentioned more than seventy times in the Bible. Jesus himself was called the *Branch of the Lord*.[57]

Leaders constantly must look for ways to expand their vision, their influence, and their contribution. There are always more possibilities than our eyes can see.

Jesus branched out.

Question
What are your current mental boundaries?

Question
Do you have a territory staked out that you can branch out into?

Question

What are your plans for expanding your influence,
your territories, and your contribution?

He Was Bold

Jesus did not mumble or whisper his message. He did not discuss for hours the safest approach for doing something. He did not go through countless committees to get permission to make a statement. He was bold.

He shouted. He stomped. He flung tables and chairs. He cried. He groaned. Everything he did made a statement about what he saw his mission to be. He crashed into people's consciousness with deeds, attitudes, and actions that had never been done, seen, or even heard of before. One could say he used his very blood to paint his message. That was how bold he was.

Understanding that authority must be assumed within

before it can be recognized externally, Jesus boldly took his authority. He did not wait until he had the total picture. He did not wait until there was a cloudless sky. He flew his banner high and carried it on a day-to-day basis. He took the canvas of his life and painted a message big enough, bold enough, and bright enough for everyone to see.

He walked into the temple as a twelve-year-old and started teaching. He stormed into the temple as an adult and turned things upside down. He called a spade a spade and apologized to no one — not out of arrogance, but out of boldness and clarity.

A magazine article recently featured the story of a couple who set sail across the Pacific Ocean on a small ship. One night a terrific storm arose. The ship tossed and bobbed, finally capsizing. The woman survived to tell the tale, but the man did not. What is interesting is that the woman said she had sensed the danger and had warned her companion. He refused to listen to her, and the boat went down. In the article she actually berated herself for not taking more power in the dangerous situation before tragedy struck. "My life was at stake, too, but because he was the *captain* I felt it wasn't my place to argue too much." She regretfully said at one point, "I should have been more adamant. I should have been more bold. Perhaps if I had been, the boat would not have sunk, and there would be two of us alive today."

What is the cost of timidity? What are the rewards of being bold? My dad used to say "He who hesitates is lost." My friend Catherine's favorite saying is "Not to decide is to decide."

Franklin Delano Roosevelt was warned by his staff that his plans to end the Depression were too large, too costly, and too rough. "Well," he thundered, "maybe they aren't perfect in every way. But, by God, we've got to do something!" His administration is credited with putting this country back on its feet again. All because one leader was bold.

Jesus was bold.

Q u e s t i o n

What would you do if you were ten times bolder? Go out and do it.

Q u e s t i o n

When and what has it cost you in life *not* to be bold?

He Boiled
It Down

The Pharisees came to Jesus and said, "Summarize for us the laws of the prophets. Which law is the most important?" They expected to trick him, thinking he would surely misquote at least one of the thousands of laws and Scriptures that had accumulated up to that time. He looked at them and said, "The laws boil down to this one. Love God with all your heart and mind and soul, and your neighbor as yourself."[58] He distilled thousands of teachings, writings, and theories into one sentence. He boiled it down.

If people could understand their core values, they would save years of doubt, confusion, and misplaced energy as they try to find direction for their lives. Jesus essentially said "If you want to be happy, do these things."

Advertisers are paid to pare things down to their essence. Take the Nike advertising campaign, for example. All of Nike's factories, sales representatives, products, energies, costs, profits, and purpose were boiled down by their ad agency into three words: Just do it. The agency created an award-winning and sales-increasing campaign based on three simple words.

My friend and associate Sally Scaman admonishes the people who report to her to: "Be bright. Be brief. And then be gone."

The essence of everything the United States stands for can be boiled down to one word: freedom. We have spent the last two hundred years trying to perfect, define, protect, understand, and implement that word.

Leaders identify, articulate, and summarize concepts that motivate others. Most important, they boil concepts down to an understandable idea.

Jesus boiled it down.

Question

If you had to boil down your message, what would it be?

Question

How could you cut some of the fat out of your words and deeds?

He Was
Visible

❧

Jesus was God's love made visible: "And the Word became flesh and dwelt among us."[59]

Jesus spoke out from the mountaintops; he did not mutter in the valleys. He spoke in synagogues, streets, temples, gardens, and at every party he went to. He was not afraid to stand out in a crowd. When the Roman soldiers, uncertain of which man they were to grab, arrested all the disciples, Jesus stepped forward and said, "I'm the one you're looking for. Let these others go."[60]

He was willing to be God's lightning rod.

I wrote a cartoon strip for a couple of years called "Stringbean." One of the cartoons I drew showed two earthworms deep underground talking to each other. One of them says, "Hey, Mortimer, have you ever raised your head to look around out there?" The other one says, "Nope. I was taught that 'He who takes a look gets the hook.' " "Yeah," Mortimer echoes, "me, too. I learned that 'He who takes a peek gets the beak. . . . ' " After a pause, Mortimer mumbles through his wall of dirt, "Lovely day, isn't it?" The point is that the earthworms had no idea what kind of day it was because they chose to stay entombed and keep a low profile. Leaders cannot keep a low profile.

D. L. Moody was one of the greatest evangelists who ever lived. He drew crowds of tens of thousands of people every time he spoke. Once when someone asked him how he could be such a powerful speaker, he said, "Before I speak I just go out to an open place and say 'Lord, set me on fire.' "

A light should be set on a hill, not hidden under a bushel. Jesus was not a low-profile person.

He was visible.

Question
How are you visible as a leader?

Question
What are ten new ways you could increase your visibility?

He Was
Willing to Do
an End Run

❧

As quarterback, Jesus knew his game plan could not be to take the truth up the middle. Perhaps he would have preferred to have his message delivered through the Levites and the Pharisees. They already had their distribution mechanisms in place. That way was blocked, however, so Jesus did an end run. He hired the fishermen. Leaders often must use innovative means to deliver a message or accomplish a goal.

One of the stories in the Old Testament that most impressed me in terms of ingenuity was that of Absalom, a son of King David who had fallen into disgrace. David was so upset with the young man that he refused even to see him. This went on for some time, and Absalom became more and more desperate to see his father. Still, the guards would not let him in. Finally Absalom announced, "If he will not hear me, I will set his fields on fire."[61] Sure enough, Absalom set the fields ablaze. Not until then did David recognize how much he had hurt his son with his unforgiveness, and the two were reconciled.

This story brings to mind Candy Leitner, the woman who started the organization Mothers Against Drunk Driving, or MADD. This woman had complained to legislators that a convicted drunk driver with a prior history of DUIs killed her teenage daughter and walked away unscathed. Who was going to listen to a weeping mother? Unfortunately, not many. Candy Leitner did not just take her grief home and cover it up. She organized a group of mothers called MADD and set the media fields on fire. She held press conferences. She passed out red ribbons. She formed support groups. She gathered statistics. She is an example of leadership in this country — an example of what one person can do. Who do you think really changed drunk driving laws in this country? A group of congressmen and senators sitting around a bar at happy hour in Washington? No. One woman, and her team, who decided to get MADD. Candy Leitner, as with so many leaders, had to do an end run to get the job done. (Notice she did not name her group NICE: "Nurturers Influencing Congress Easily.")

If you believe you have a just cause, an important message, or a key contribution to make, you will be just as innovative as a college freshman desperate to see his girlfriend six hundred miles away. You will *get there* anyway you can.

Jesus was willing to do an end run.

Q u e s t i o n

What strategies have you been using to get your message or project through?

Q u e s t i o n

Are you willing to try another way?

Q u e s t i o n

What new approaches come to mind?

STRENGTH OF ACTION

He Took
the Long View

Cartoonist Gary Larson has a way of looking at things that keeps us from taking ourselves too seriously. One of my favorite Larson cartoons shows a very solemn and serious Indian scout leaning down with his ear to the ground. A group of intent-looking cavalry soldiers surrounds him. The Indian says, "Yep. Heap big buffalo stampede. Three, maybe four feet away."

Unlike the Indian guide, Jesus took the long view of things. That must be why he always liked to preach on top of a hill.

A famous cartoonist illustrates a creature "face to face with the second step." The creature's face is pressed against the step so closely it is unable to move up, backward, sideways, or forward without falling off. The creature is completely stuck. The message might be that the creature lost its momentum by overanalysis. The message also might be that when you are up against a step, you cannot see where the next step is leading. Sometimes opportunity is like staring at the knees of a giraffe.

The following memos illustrate the difference between long- and short-view thinking.

MEMORANDUM I

TO: JC
FROM: JI
RE: Need to take action against the Roman
      Empire

As you know, our membership is up dramatically and many are calling you the king. Isn't it time to take action on this rising swell of public opinion and eliminate the competition?

Respectfully yours,
Judas Iscariot

```
MEMORANDUM II

TO:    JC
FROM: JI
RE:    Recent action of your friend at party

As treasurer of the organization, I might point out
that one of our mission statements is to feed the
poor. The recent action of Mary, so-called Magda-
lene, of breaking an expensive bottle of ointment
and pouring it over your feet was a total waste of
shekels and sends the wrong message to our, oops,
your adoring crowd. Please encourage others in the
future to refrain from such flamboyant gestures.

Sincerely,
Judas Iscariot
```

You can imagine what Jesus' responses to these
memos would have been. To the first memo regarding an
uprising against Rome, Jesus simply said, "My kingdom
is not of this world." To the second memo he replied, "The
poor shall always be here. What she has done is prepare
my path with love and deep affection. In fact, she has
shown so much pure love that wherever my story is told,
her name and this deed will be remembered."[62]

Mary Magdalene's name and deed are recounted in all four of the Gospels, while Judas became synonymous with the word *traitor*. Judas was the one who always encouraged the short view of things.

Jesus took the long view.

Question

What is the long view of your leadership plan?

Question

How does your leadership plan impact the future?

He Knew That
No One Could
Ruin His Plans

Consider how Jesus must have felt when one of his beloved staff turned against him. This experience is common to many of us in business, in friendship, and in romance. But even when Judas betrayed him,[63] Jesus did not fail. With all the Machiavellian, sinister forces of evil piled up against him, Jesus did not fail. He was able to take the hit and keep on going. Nobody can keep you down unless *you* decide not to rise again.

Betrayals, bosses with bad news, angry ex-partners, and loans that do not come through . . . all of these are part of life's drama. But leaders do not quit when they suffer a loss. They press on for the victory.

Jesus knew that no one could ruin his plans.

Question

What recent loss or betrayal have you suffered that might be causing you to want to give up?

Question

If you give up, who will *really* be the reason for your defeat?

He Practiced the
WOWSE Concept

The acronym WOWSE became a vital affirmation for me when I was starting my company. Like too many others, I had tried to get assistance from banks and was continually turned down. Every time I was rejected, I would say to myself "WOWSE," which means "With or Without Someone Else." "I will build this company with or without someone else," I would repeat to myself as I licked my wounds.

As time went on, more and more people did step forward to help me. But the first few years were rough, at least as far as financing was concerned. This turned out to be a blessing, since I had to learn rather quickly how to generate cash flow. (My affirmation in those days was "WOWSE." My mother's was "Please God, send her cash flow.")

A leader must be so committed to a project that she is willing to do it with or without someone else. David did not turn to see if the troops were following him when he went out to meet Goliath. He was not even a king but merely a shepherd boy at the time he took on the giant. He became king after he went out alone.

Jesus was committed to healing, teaching, and preaching regardless of whether his crew came along. He would have done the job set before him with or without Peter and Mary Magdalene. One of my partners, Dominic, impressed me when I saw him handle the mail and make cold calls for a business in which he was the majority owner. A very wealthy man who employed more than 350 people, here he was at the post office hand-stamping 1,500 pieces of mail. "Dominic," I said, "why not send one of the staff to do that?" "Everyone else was in meetings," he said good-naturedly, "and this mail had to go out today."

Later he told me he had been raised on a farm where everybody pitched in to do whatever needed to be done. "When a cow needed milking, my dad didn't care whose turn it was to milk it — the job just had to get done."

Businesses would run much smoother if everyone felt this way. The lack of this "just get the job done" attitude

STRENGTH OF ACTION

is one of the reasons true customer service is in such critical shortage and demand. People are so busy checking their job descriptions that they do not have time to do the work they need to do. One of the primary rules of good business management is that managers should not ask their employees to do anything *they* are not willing to do. Time is wasted when managers wait for help to arrive.

Eleanor Roosevelt, one of the greatest leaders of our time, personally supported a number of students financially. I once read an article that said a young man remembered getting checks for $75 a month, made and signed by Eleanor Roosevelt on her personal account. He said he received those checks for years, even after she ceased to be the First Lady.

It would have been much easier for her to refer him to some giant scholarship committee, maybe even write him a nice recommendation letter. However, she was personally committed to education and supporting students she felt were worthy. She supported more than twenty-five students out of her personal funds. She was willing to help the students *with or without someone else*.

Jesus practiced the WOWSE concept.

Question

What commitment are you willing to make happen with or without someone else?

Question

Who and what, besides yourself, have you been supporting with your personal "bank account"?

He Took
One Step
at a Time

A famous author and philanthropist, Louise Hay, was asked what led her to her great work. She said, "It was simple. I just did the next thing in front of me and helped out where I could." She now owns a publishing company, a best-selling book and tape series, and a house by the ocean. These are all merely benefits of her taking one step at a time, and helping out where she could.

The temptation to have everything done all at once and perfectly often leads to procrastination, inactivity, or outright paralysis. Yet typically, so much needs to be done that good leaders and managers are constantly encouraging their team to be forward-thinking in their approach and steady in their actions.

A friend of mine named Bob Campion, who is charged with renovating and upgrading sometimes as many as fifteen rural health facilities at once, was summoned to a staff meeting in Florida. He told his boss, Bill, "If you could just give me one more week, I will have all my ducks in a row." Bill replied, "We don't have time for that, Bob. Just bring your crackers, and we'll line up the ducks together."

As my mother once admonished me, "Honey, even if you're going to fall, you can always fall forward." Deep water is where the fish really are. Leaders are constantly thrown into deep waters.

Leadership does not come with detail-filled, certified maps . . . only a general sense of directions.

Even Jesus, clear as he was about his calling, had to get his instructions one day at a time. One time he was told to wait, another time to go.

One of my business advisors told me about a friend of his who is now living his dream: owning and running a resort hotel in Hawaii. "Do you know how he got there?" he asked. "By flipping pancakes . . . one flip at a time." This man's dream was to own a hotel, but he did not have any money. He signed on as a cook at a pancake house and was soon promoted to manager. Then he and the owner teamed up and bought another pancake house and another. It was not long before their little pancake house real estate empire had been sold and turned into a resort hotel in Hawaii. "Ron," I said, laughing, "he was flipping pancake *restaurants*, not flipping pancakes." "Well"—he grinned—"you get the point. He started out as a cook and took one step at a time."

And so when I would come to him full of eagerness and frustration about what my next step could be and asking a thousand questions about how was I ever going to get there, Ron would smile at me and say, "Flip . . . flip . . . flip," making little pancake motions with his hands.

Jesus took one step at a time.

Question

Do you need to see the whole picture before you can move forward?

Question

Can you name several leaders who took a step without knowing where they were going?

He Took
His Staff
in Hand

Jesus took his staff in hand when he said, "Greater things than I have done shall you do." He took his staff in hand when he said, "You have the right to use my name to do what must be done."

Taking one's staff in hand means that there must be unity of purpose. Leaders must know and use existing resources to accomplish a deed. Their resources must be in agreement and alignment with their goals so that they work hand in hand to accomplish the deed. Leaders must direct their resources with concentration and the intention to succeed.

As a child, I was fascinated by Cecil B. De Mille's movie *The Ten Commandments*. In it Moses never went anywhere without a physical staff in his hand, whether he was confronting the belligerent Pharaoh or shepherding the scared and complaining Israelites. He knew that "staff" had power in it. It turned into a snake at the Pharaoh's feet. It turned into a rock smasher and a Red Sea divider in the wilderness. When faced with difficult situations, Moses took his staff in hand and used it with authority, conviction, and power.

Moses did not use his staff as a fishing pole to support some dangling bait. This is how office staffs are all too often used, however. The fishing-pole mentality becomes evident when a receptionist cannot state what the mission of the company is or when there is high turnover of personnel. A friend of mine, who is an attorney, helped twenty physicians break away from their hospital and set up their own corporation. When I asked her why the doctors left, she replied, "They felt they were just being used as bait for the larger group. They did not feel that they were being treated with respect." That is how management often views and treats sales force, its support staff, or even its own customers — as bait for bigger deals.

Your customers are also part of your staff. They can be your most viable sales force.

It is important first to convince your people of your

mission statement and then to educate them thoroughly and wisely in the inspirational aspect of what you and they are doing. When the time comes, you will be better able to direct them with authority.

I once counseled a company that was so rife with competition and infighting that its members had obviously forgotten their mission. I said, "While you are arguing over how to slice the pie, your competitor is walking off with the kitchen." Their leader had let the staff de-focus and thus disintegrate.

Jesus had a huge task, but he accomplished what he set out to do. He took his staff in hand. He said, "Go now, and teach as you've been taught, and demonstrate what you have learned."

Jesus took his staff in hand.

Question

When have you taken your staff in hand and used its power to accomplish something?

Question

What decision are you delaying because you are subconsciously waiting for reinforcements?

Question

What keeps you from taking your staff in hand and addressing the situation in a forceful, faith-filled, and assertive way?

He Served Only
the Best Wine

I recently visited relatives of a friend of mine who had their living room furniture covered with plastic. "Twenty years and this sofa is still as good as new." Susan's mother beamed. Picturing New York's sweltering heat, I asked Susan, "What did you do in the summer?" "We stayed out of the living room," she replied with a sigh. Then who was the sofa for?

Jesus did not keep himself in reserve. The first miracle that Jesus performed was turning water into wine at a wedding. Jesus poured out the best of his affection freely to all he encountered.

This is an important action skill because we so often

bestow affection in small droplets for people. Probably we have all encountered that professor who said no one deserved an A, or the boss who could never say "Well done."

I met somebody who displayed affectionate spontaneity when I started a new job in Atlanta. When I was introduced to the secretary, she looked up from her desk and said instantly, "Oh! I hope you work here forever!" She did not know me, but she wanted to make me her friend. She had already decided to love me before I walked in the door. I wish more people were able to be affectionate spontaneously. Unfortunately, many of us are like the Olympic judges measuring people's performance in tenths of a point before we open up our hearts to them.

Why do we wait to serve the wine? Jesus, like so many young people today, never reached the age of forty. Perhaps knowing that he wouldn't be here long is what caused him to serve the best wine first. He gave the wine freely to anyone who wanted it. He poured out the best of himself to all he encountered.

He served only the best wine.

Question

What in your life still has plastic on it, being saved for some special occasion?

Question

How often do you withhold love and affection until someone has "earned" it?

He Changed
the Unit of
Measurement

Perhaps the most important thing a leader can do is to change the unit of measurement. Jesus constantly said, "It has been written . . . *but* I say . . ." He was changing the units of measurements — of holiness, of the requirements for entrance into God's presence . . . of how we measure growth and worth in the human race. It is not about the volume of your prayers, it is about the depth of them. It is not about how good you look, it is how you treat the lilies.

All of us are slaves to our ideas, and the concepts we have of success are what drive us. One of the greatest conflicts in consciousness I have had comes from the fact that my mother was an artist and my father was a salesman. Mom would paint a painting, and Dad would admire it briefly, and then say, "What do you think you could sell it for?" (This is probably why I went into advertising. I tell people I was bred for it.) I fully understand why my mother did not get out her brushes seriously until he was out of town. His overarching unit of measure kept her creative spirit in check.

Clichés die hard, yet when men are measured in terms of their money and women are measured in terms of their looks, we have a long way to go in creating a sense of values for our children. I find beauty pageants to be amazing cultural events. Can you imagine the message we are sending children of both sexes when we have a panel of judges rating women in various states of makeup and undress — rating them in terms of tenths of a point? "Here comes Miss New Jersey, Bud. I give her a 9.6." No wonder we have ten-and eleven-year-old girls fainting in math class because they are dieting, trying to lose ten pounds. Women must not be measured and weighed like cattle. Yet even today, when magazines talk about models, they give their height and weight. Men, too, must not be measured in terms of how much money they have in the bank. I get amused when magazines like *Forbes* quote someone's "net worth." Does that mean that a person worth X.X billion is worth more than a child with a quarter in his pocket? Sounds ridiculous, doesn't it? Yet watch how people with money are treated compared to those who have none. It's all because of our cultural units of measurement.

We are slaves to our beliefs . . . sold to our particular units of measurement.

I am a member of the World Business Academy, which is dedicated to changing the units of measurement in businesses and nations. Comprised of business executives and leaders, this group meets regularly in city chapters and at annual retreats to dialogue about how to change paradigms in business. At a recent convention in Dallas, Texas, one of the speakers stated that the United Nations is considering ways to measure nations' progress with indices that would not be limited to gross national product or pure economic output, but would also include such factors as the status of women and children and environmental sensitivity. The premise of the World Business Academy is that when profit is the only measurement of success in business, the result will be exploitation of resources. This money measurement has had drastic effects on the sustainability of the planet and on the spiritual development of human beings.

Let's turn for a moment to Hollywood and its profit-tracking measurements. I have read that action movies sell more, both here and overseas. Therefore, we have a plethora of movies that dynamite and maim and use high kicks to paralyze and destroy. Today I read that the wizardry of computer technology is being put to "high use." Children now can purchase a video game that allows the victor to either "tear the heart out" or "pull the spine out" of his defeated opponent. Apparently several million dollars and a great deal of thought have gone into planning this sure-to-be-profitable children's game.

Is this the best that we can do? With all the gifts at our command and disposal, with all the centuries of technological advances, is this what we offer our Creator and, in our children, our Creative future?

Using money as the only "unit of measurement" seems a surefire way to decadence. Jesus said something specifically to this effect: "Using money as the only unit of measurement is the root of all evil. . . ."

It is time for us — for all of us — to change the unit of measurement, how we measure success, how we measure progress, and how we measure ourselves.

Jesus changed the unit of measurement.

Question
Currently what unit of measurement are you using to determine you worth? Is it money? Is it achieve-

ments? Is it your weight? The number of cars you have? What is it?

Question

What units of measurement would you like to change?

He Troubled
Himself on
Behalf of Others

In one of the books of the Old Testament, God says (through Jeremiah), "This is what I have against you — that you have not troubled yourself on my behalf."

In a recent essay in *U.S. News & World Report*, John Leo states that today many people treat God as a hobby. No relationship can survive when one or both parties start treating each other casually and stop troubling themselves on the other's behalf.

I believe that God yearns to have an intense and even romantic relationship with each one of us. After all, Jesus came here looking for his "Bride." And one of the main elements of romance is the trouble the romancer goes to on behalf of the romancee. Hiring mariachi bands to sing beneath balconies, sky-writing "Ellen, will you marry me?" sending a dozen roses after each week's anniversary are all actions that show that someone went to a lot of trouble to demonstrate love and affection. Yet so often we treat God like that lonely housewife who is supposed to know her husband loves her simply because he eats her cooking.

God was said to have loved King David so much because David loved God back totally, intensely, and passionately. What are the Psalms, really, but love songs to God? David and Jonathan were friends who went out of their way to show love for one another. Naomi and Ruth demonstrated a love between women that was so strong they were willing to be uprooted on the other's behalf. In fact, it is their "vows" that are often repeated in traditional weddings today: "Whither thou goest, I will go. Thy people will be my people. Whither thou liest, I also will lie. And where you are buried, I also will be buried. . . ."

I believe if we look closely at all the biblical heroes and heroines, the common thread is simply that they troubled themselves on God's behalf.

If you think that God isn't interested or doesn't need our spontaneous and personal display of affection, then you haven't read the Song of Solomon or the story about Mary Magdalene when she poured precious ointment over Jesus' feet. He was so touched by her expensive and expansive display of affection that he decreed her act of love would be told wherever his story was told. Jesus himself needed to hear people declare their feelings for him — out loud. "Do you love me, Peter?" was an honest and sincere question from a waiting heart.

The way we can show our love for God does not require any elaborate formula. Jesus outlined it quite clearly. "If you have done it for any of these, even the least of these my people, you have done it unto me." Forget the fancy ceremonies . . . loud prayers in the marketplace . . . showy checks written out on TV. Jesus said the way to show you love God is to treat every soul you meet as if she or he were the very own child of God. He said even if we bring someone a glass of water, we will not lose our reward.

I once met a woman who owns a phenomenally successful executive recruiting company. When I asked her what her secret was, she said, "It's simple. Whenever the phone rings, I say to myself, 'That's God on the line,' and then I think about all the ways I can serve that person. . . ."

If we have become a people of mediocrity, it is because we have stopped troubling ourselves on God's behalf.

Jesus troubled himself on God's behalf, and on the behalf of others.

Question

How do you trouble yourself on God's behalf?

Question

Who is troubling her- or himself on your behalf?

He Trained
His Replacements

I personally witnessed the downfall of an executive director who had ruled a huge organization for nearly twelve
years, largely through smoke and mirrors. When his incompetence finally came collapsing down upon him and
he was relieved of his command, there was quite a mess
to clean up. The problem was, it wasn't just his incompetence that had to be corrected. He had multiplied himself
by hiring people who were far less qualified, and hence
less of a threat, to him in every area. This organization
had a core of incompetence that, like a cancer, had infil-
trated every department and nearly caused the demise of
the entire organization.

By contrast, Jesus as a CEO was eager and intent upon hiring people he felt could replace him. "Greater things than I have done shall you do," he promised. Jesus did not hoard or guard the power of his office. He kept teaching and sharing and demonstrating it so team members would learn that they, too, had the power to do what he had done.

In order for him to be so generous with his power, Jesus obviously had to have been extremely secure. He repeatedly affirmed and clearly understood his standing with "the Chairman of the Board." He never doubted that, when it was all over, he would be sitting at the Head Table. His job was to fill that table and make sure others were sitting with him.

Florence Littauer is an amazing woman who has written over thirteen books, one of which, *Personality Plus*, has sold over 300,000 copies. I attended one of her seminars and was surprised when she came on stage with about twenty-six other authors — each of whom she had helped to write their *own* books. She stood there with all those authors and said, "If you think I am proudest of my books, you are wrong. I am most proud of the people I have helped to become writers themselves." She didn't define her success in terms of her products, but in terms of the people she had trained. Had she been an insecure author, she might have tried to lessen the competition. But in fact, she was busy training her replacements.

Jesus trained his replacements.

Question

What would be the benefits of replacing yourself on the job?

Question

Are you secure with your place at the Head Table? As King David wrote in Psalm 16:5 "Lord, you, and you only, hold my lot secure." If that is so, then there is no need to hoard the power. All reservations have been made in your name and will be honored.

He Said
"Why *Not* Me?"

W hen something bad happens to us, one of the first thoughts we have is usually "Why me, Lord?" As the old man Tevye moans in the play *Fiddler on the Roof*, "I know we're the Chosen People, God, but can't you choose somebody else part of the time?"

Yet a key ingredient of leadership and maturity is to be able to say "Why not me?" My friend Catherine rolls her eyes when she hears testimonies on television about how God spared someone from a horrible plane crash or a pile-up on the freeway. "Does that mean that God didn't love the people who were in the crash?" she asks incredulously. The very idea that God blesses only the good and punishes only the evil leads immediately to the question "Then what did Jesus do to cause him to die so young and so painfully?" God is much bigger than our understanding of good and bad, and has an eternal plan that none of us grasps totally. In fact, the willingness to enter into whatever God wants is one of the hallmarks of spiritual leadership.

Jesus told the story about a wealthy landowner who entrusted his vineyards to a certain group of people. The landowner sent emissary after emissary to the far country to see how his land was faring, only to have them return with reports of being ignored, mistreated, and even beaten and stoned. At this point I can just see Jesus, as the landowner's eldest son, stepping up and saying "Father, why not send me?"

David also uttered these words when all the other Israelites were trembling in their tents as the giant Goliath boomed out his insults and challenges. "No one else is willing to go out there. Why not me?"

The why-not-me question applies equally to the blessing side of the equation. If you study some of the most successful athletes or entrepreneurs, you will undoubtedly find that at some point they looked at other people who were experiencing success and said "Why not me?"

A year ago my mother went to visit an art gallery in Sedona, Arizona. After Mom oohed and ahhed about how lucky the woman working there was to live in such a hauntingly beautiful part of the country, the woman said, "Why don't you move here?" Mom immediately replied that she didn't think she could afford to live there. The woman laughed and said, "You think I'm made of money? No way. But one day I decided that this is where I wanted to live, so I up and moved here. You can, too." Then she gave her a list of real estate offices to visit. On the way home Mom kept saying to herself "That woman lives in Sedona. Why not me?" She went home to El Paso, praying the whole way, put her home of thirty-four years on the market, sold it that day to a man who had always admired it, and within sixty days was sipping tea on her new balcony in Sedona.

Lately one of my mental exercises is to look at people who are doing more of what I really want to be doing and realizing "They are doing this. Why not me?" This is not done with envy, jealousy, or malice. Mostly it is about recognizing that none of us is to a caste system born, and that we, too, can delight in the benefits and the banquets of life.

Jesus was in effect a walking invitation to a Great Banquet. And the only requirement for attendance is that the person accept the invitation. "Moses is going. David is going. Queen Esther is going. Jeremiah is going. The whole gang's going to be there.

"Why not me?"

Question

Do you often feel envy about someone else's success?

Question

What could *you* do to attain that success?

He Let
It Go

Perhaps Jesus' ultimate act of faith was not so much in coming to earth as in leaving it. After a lifetime of preparation and only three years of implementation and training, he had to look at his mission and then let it go. "It is finished," he said in his dying breath. And then he let it go.

When you have done everything humanly possible — with a project, with a business, with a relationship — then the only thing left to do is to let it go.

In one of the movies about Indiana Jones, he and his father are pursuing the Holy Grail. After many adventures and heartaches, Indiana is finally at the precipice —

about to grasp the very item he and his father have been searching for. And yet, so precarious is his position on the cliff that his father realizes if Indiana retrieves the grail, he will lose his balance and fall into the pit below. As Indiana is about to lift up the prize, his father whispers, "Let it go." There is a long pause, and you can see the anguish in Indiana's face. Have they come all this way for nothing? Can't he finally grasp the treasure they've been searching for? Can't he finally make his father proud of him? Another second passes, and his father takes his arm and says more firmly, "Indiana, let it go."

Indiana does as he is instructed, and the audience gasps. It is so un-Indiana like — so un-American, so un-Hollywood — that they should come all this way for nothing. And yet almost instantly the audience begins to realize that the trip wasn't about getting the grail. It was about spending time together on the journey — about being all tied up and facing death together and emerging with a stronger relationship. *That* was the prize.

I wonder how often God is whispering to us "Let it go." Just as in the movie, our Father has been with us on the journey and perhaps is trying to tell us that, in this particular circumstance, to grasp the prize might cause us to lose our balance and tumble into a pit. It is then we can feel Him tugging at us, whispering "Let it go. It is finished. Let it go."

Jesus let it go.

Question

What project or relationship have you been hanging on to so tightly that it is causing you to lose your balance?

Question

If indeed you could hear God whispering "Let it go," would you?

Question

If you did, what might you have gained on the journey that was the real prize?

He Rose
Above It All

Leaders must be able to rise above controversies, jealousies, petty personal attacks, and ego slights, real or imagined, in order to accomplish anything of worth.

One of the people I have had the pleasure of working with is a CEO at an osteopathic hospital. After a meeting in which some new directions for the hospital were presented, several of the mid-level managers grew concerned about the potential upset it might have to those who were used to doing things as before. This leader calmly listened to their fears (for the fourteenth time) and then turned to the person in charge of implementing the changes and said simply, "Proceed as planned." The simple directive indicated that, as captain, he had set his sights on the goal and wasn't about to be drawn off course by fractionary arguments among the crew. He was acting on his aerial view.

When I look at people occupying powerful seats in Congress and the presidency itself, I do not forget the many attacks, vilifications, insults, and opposition they endured in order to attain their powerful status. Influence doesn't come easily.

Jesus rose above it all by keeping a heavenly perspective. To be "in the world, yet not of it" means rising above it all. He said, "When I am lifted up I will draw all people to me." Again, he was telling us about the power inherent in taking an aerial view. Driving home late one afternoon, I saw an intriguing sight. The Miramar Naval Air Station was having its annual air show. Cars had stopped all along the freeway to watch the silver planes' fantastic dips, twists, twirls, and dives. There, in a bare eucalyptus tree, sat a hawk — watching the planes put on their show. She seemed so calm and centered in the midst of the thunderous display.

In fact, the hawk seemed thoughtful. It was as if she were thinking "I, too, have the power to fly — with equal grace and measure. After the noise is over, I will rise and fly away — still master of all I see."

Jesus, despite all the thunderous noise around him, maintained confidence in his wings and his perspective.

He rose above it all.

Question

What "fray" are you involved in that you could "rise above" by taking an aerial view?

Question

Who represents thunderous, seemingly more powerful "competition" to you?

He Came to
Be a Blessing

Sandra Marleen Harrison is a dear friend who has known me over twenty years. Having known me from the time I was a college student into my years as a businesswoman, she has listened to my list of goals recited ad nauseam over the phone. While mine have often changed depending on market conditions, hers have always remained the same. She says her only goal in life is simply "To be a blessing."

This used to frustrate me tremendously, mostly because it kept her end of the conversation so short. How do you develop an action plan and benchmarks for that kind of goal? Really, at times she was not much fun to strategize with.

And yet, as I have grown, I find that her goal is becoming more and more my own. "To be a blessing." I remember being uncertain one night after having just secured a year-long contract for a client — the largest retainer I had ever obtained. And though I had researched and worked for six months to get it, the minute that executive board said "You are hired," I must admit I experienced a moment of fear. What if I couldn't live up to their expectations — expectations that I had created by my presentation and promises? What if these people's hard-earned money and trust was going to go down the drain because of some error or omission I might unknowingly make? That night I picked up the Gideon Bible, and it opened to a verse I had never seen before.

It was from Proverbs 3:18, talking about Wisdom, and it read, "She is a tree of life to all who lay hold of her branches. Happy are all who *retaineth* her." And then I realized that was what I wanted more than anything else: to be a blessing to them, in ways that would far surpass the stipulations of the contract.

If you track the result of Jesus' energy on earth, everything bloomed, was healed, or came to life in his presence. (The only exceptions were the fig tree, the Pharisees, and Judas, which sounds like the title for a song.)

In the Old and New Testaments there are so many

beautiful passages of what blessings look like: of rivers running where once only deserts were, of lions laying down with lambs, of fields of wheat swaying and singing in the breeze, of every person having her own shade and fruit tree. . . .

Isn't it interesting that when something bad happens, the first words out of our mouths are often curses? And many of them invoke God's and Jesus' name! Who switched the connection? And how many blessing words do we know? And how often do we use them?

Jesus came to bless, not to curse. To heal. To bring life, and bring it abundantly. To make the crooked places straight. To wipe away our tears and fears.

He came to be a blessing.

Question
How could you be more of a blessing to others?

Question
What do blessings look like?

Question
Who has blessed you, and how?

He Was a
Turnaround
Specialist

❧

In almost every situation in which Jesus found himself, his job was to turn things around. In fact, that was his specialty.

"The people have forgotten who I am. Turn this around.

"There is a little girl dying. Turn this around.

"People are dishonoring the temple. Turn this around."

If people were sitting in ashes, his job was to give them a garland of joy. The list goes on and on of the turnaround things he was sent to do. He did not have nor did he take the luxury of looking at difficult situations and saying "Well, politically it would be wise for me to just go with the flow here. . . ." In fact, he said at one point, "I didn't come to bring peace. I came to bring a sword."

In each instance his turnaround technique was different. He followed no set formula. If he had, the famous put-mud-in-your-eye-from-the-river cure for blindness would be marketed through direct mail today. He didn't come to give us formulas. He came to give us a new mind-set — one that has a turnaround mentality. In fact, the word *repent* means to turn around.

We are each called to be turnaround specialists. When we are faced with difficult situations, we should rejoice, because that's what we're here for. My friend Catherine and I went to a motivational talk Dr. Norman Vincent Peale gave years ago. There he said, "When you see a problem coming down the road, holler 'Hello, Problem! Where have you been? I've been training for you all my life!' "

Society is filled with turnaround specialists. A nurse at a hospice comforts a family, spending time answering their questions about death in detail, and slowly the anxiety they were feeling disappears. . . . A teacher takes a special interest in a child who is blind, and has been labeled "mentally retarded" only to have Helen Keller grow into a woman who inspires millions. A young couple adopts a child from a foster program, and slowly the frightened boy gets a new, turned-around image of what real parental love came be.

Physicians reverse the progress of a disease. Artists take empty canvases and turn them into paintings that take your breath away. Entrepreneurs take an area of abandoned warehouses and adult bookstores and turn it into a thriving, bustling, revitalized downtown. A woman writes a book about slavery in the South, and *Uncle Tom's Cabin* fuels a war that changes America forever.

We each have within us the power to turn things around. In fact, if Jesus is our coach and Lord, it should be our specialty.

He turned things around.

Question

What situation in your workplace, your community, or the world would you like to see turned around?

Question

When have you successfully turned something around in the past? How did you do it?

He Knew
He Was
Not Alone

Jesus had a sense of companionship with the divine source of his being, a source that not only knew him intimately but cared for him as well.

Jesus spoke about God as Father not to perpetuate the image of a patriarchal power chain so much as to imply a birthing from, a presence of nurturing and intense watchfulness, a deep pride of creation. An immutable connection. Love.

As much as I appreciate the power we each have within ourselves to create our destinies, I cannot escape the notion that above us hovers a benevolent, all-knowing, and intensely kind-full presence . . . a personality of Good.

I cannot be comforted by the thought of some Vast Neutral Oversoul that regards me as merely a speck of light on a diamond-studded ocean.

As much as I desire independence and take pride in stretching my wings, I want to know that Someone is watching and cares about every move I make. I want a God who knows my middle name.

Once I wrote a poem entitled "Net" that reads:

There is a net under us all.
Sometimes we dance
and sometimes
we fall.
And
there is a net
under us all.

Jesus had this sense of life. In fact, if you looked at what drove him — especially on his darker days — it was his desire to please his Father . . . a desire to return to this very intense and personal embrace again.

My mother shared with me last night how, in a state of stress, she prayed desperately for a profound truth from the Lord.

"Do you know what I heard Him saying to me?" she asked. " 'Let's dance,' He said. 'Let's dance.' "

God loves to dance.

God invites us to join the movement, the swaying, the feeling of being in harmony with something larger than ourselves. It is a rare group that can stand linked arm in arm in a circle and not begin to sway.

In the book *The Lives of a Cell*, author Lewis Thomas speculates that perhaps in the near future we might try to make contact with alien beings. The dilemma becomes what do we say to them? What should form our giant Hello?

Thomas decides that we should broadcast Bach, "even though it would be bragging."

Thomas also informs us that all of earth is continually humming . . . that even earthworms make drumming sounds, and termites hit a staccato note that no one can find reason for even after years of observation.

Jesus heard the humming, too. He said the rocks and trees can sing — that they will do so and have been.

All of this for one simple reason: We are not alone.

My mother wrote this poem shortly after moving to Sedona, Arizona.

MIDNIGHT STARS
by Irene A. Jones

I've wondered these days
why you brought me here, Lord . . .
far from my beloved ones

to this strange enchanted place . . .
alone for now . . . alone.

 Wondering still I stepped out
into the cold winter night,
Looked to the midnight skies
and there . . . the glory of the Lord
shone round about me!

 I know the answer . . . for I saw
heaven's
stars . . . millions . . . so many I could
only stand in awe . . .
overcome by stars . . . planets . . .
galaxies . . . and then . . . a falling star!

 For this I came . . . beauty to behold
undimmed by raw city lights;
and in the darkling silence
heard Brother Coyote sing
his lonesome song
to the star-kissed night.

 Tears came that I should be so
blessed . . .
that you would light my path, Lord . . .
Your angels guide my steps.
Alone? No. You are with me, I know.

My heart sings a solo . . . "Silent night,
holy night, all is so calm, all is so
bright,
round your children bathed
in star's light . . .
O holy night. O holy, holy night."

Jesus knew he was not alone.

Question

Do you feel a Higher Power caring for you in a personal way?

Question

If you were to give God a personal nickname, what would it be? Does this thought offend you? If so, why?

STRENGTH OF RELATIONSHIPS

Love the Lord your God with all your heart and soul and mind and strength, and your neighbor as yourself. On this, hang all the law and the prophets.

MATTHEW 22:37-39

He Gave Them a Vision of Something Larger than Themselves

Jesus walked up to the fishermen and said, "Follow me, and I will make you fishers of men."[64] They dropped their nets and followed him. He met a woman at a well and said, "Follow me, and you will never be thirsty again."[65] She dropped her bucket and ran to get all of her friends.

History repeatedly has shown that people hunger for something larger than themselves. Leaders who offer that will have no shortage of followers. In fact, *higher purpose* is such a vital ingredient to the human psyche that a Scripture says "Where there is no vision, the people perish."[66]

Studies show that people will work harder and longer

on projects when they understand the overall significance of their individual contribution. The study most often quoted is that of airplane workers who were divided into two groups. Members of one group simply did what they were told to do, while the other group's members were taken to the engineering lab and shown how their particular pieces were part of a magnificent jet that would fly higher and faster than any jet had ever flown before. Without any additional incentive, the second group's productivity soared. They knew how important their contribution was to a larger plan.

Today stores and companies print their mission statements on their literature to inform the public about why they exist. A flyer by a local jeweler reads: "My mission is to create magnificent jeweled pieces that bring beauty to the soul." She feels a higher calling with her work.

Everyone has heard or read about the superhuman strength that possesses a person who suddenly needs to lift a truck off a fallen buddy or leap into flames to save a child. These events may seem extraordinary and dramatic, but they demonstrate an important fact. When we are called on to do something beyond the thought of our own survival, special energy comes to our aid. A leader can tap into this special energy by showing staffers the long-lasting significance of what they are doing.

Jesus clearly and consistently conveyed to his staff the significance of what they were doing. He spoke long and often about the calling, and they could feel and see the long-lasting benefits of their work with him. They were changing people's lives for the good. They were working for something beyond themselves.

Leaders, both humane and inhumane, have been able to tap into this special human need. History is full of stories of people who gave their lives for a cause that was noble and holy in their eyes. Perhaps it is because deep down, we know that we are made of stardust, not just dust, and are willing to give up what we have on earth in order to approach the heavens from whence we came.

Jesus gave them a vision of something larger than themselves.

Question

What would your employees answer if asked, "What is your job?" And more important: "Why is your job significant?"

Question

Do you clearly communicate to your staff the higher purpose for their activities?

He Beheld
Them

ocus is one of the key attributes of a leader, and nowhere is it more powerful when applied to and on behalf of another human being.

When a truly charismatic leader is introduced to someone, the leader will *behold* that person. "And Jesus beheld the man, and looking at him, loved him."[67] The moment of introduction is treated as a holy moment. There is long and direct eye contact, and the leader focuses concentration on that person so that she or he feels like the most important person in the room. It is no coincidence that leaders like this often have such a high recall of names. They focus on that person in that moment.

To behold someone means to *be* fully centered and to *hold*, or embrace, a person in that moment. The Omega leader beholds his or her people daily. Scientifically we are each a new creation every day. Many of our cells replace themselves on a daily basis. Therefore, what appears to be the same may not really *be* the same.

Another reason the Omega leader beholds each person is because one of God's favorite games is *disguise*. Blessings masquerade as problems, kings and queens come clothed in rags, and more than one person has "entertained angels unaware."[68]

To illustrate the power of someone viewing you in a certain light, think about what it is like to go back home. I have observed powerful professionals suddenly start acting like eight-year-olds when confronted with the raised eyebrow of a parent. People who command the respect of entire corporations suddenly can be reduced to whining masses of helplessness. Often parents do not see us as the adults we are today but as the children we once were. This viewpoint can literally throw us — in terms of behavior — back in time.

People respond to how you behold them in your consciousness. You don't have to say anything, they can sense how you perceive them. Too often we only view people in terms of our needs and hidden agendas.

The words that are placed after our names — our titles — establish our boundaries. That is why people often will not do anything beyond their job descriptions. A secretary, for example, might always act like a secretary; whereas an assistant vice president actually might do the same tasks but will take more risks and strive to accomplish higher goals. How we view or "title" others often sets their boundaries in limiting or unlimiting ways.

People flocked to Jesus because he did not see them as black or white, rich or poor, male or female. He saw them as brothers and sisters — family related by blood. Equals with equal rights and responsibilities.[69]

He beheld them.

Question

Do you see your staff as new creations every day, or do you see them as their job descriptions?

Question

How much concentrated, focused time do you spend *beholding* your employees each day?

Question

What hidden qualities do each of your employees have that are just waiting to be discovered?

He Said

"Yes"

～⚬～

One of the most phenomenal people I know is a woman named Lawreve Widmar. She was raised on a ranch in Mexico and is the mother of thirteen children. She has sparkling blue eyes and a million-dollar smile.

Lawreve has taught me many principles about unconditional love. After her first husband died, she married Siegfried. At first she was unprepared for the whirlwind schedule he kept as an international designer. He would come home and ask, "Can you come with me to Mexico City in two hours?" She finally decided that no matter what he asked her, or when, she would say yes.

She raised her thirteen children in such a way that

Siegfried would not be disturbed or distracted from his work. "He had such artistic sensibilities that I couldn't bear to see them ruffled," she said. So when Siegfried made a request of her, she just said yes. She is now a corporate vice president, and Siegfried willingly says yes when she asks him to accompany her on last-minute business trips.

Jesus said yes. "Yes, I will come to your party. Yes, I will show you where my house is. Yes, I will meet your mother-in-law. Yes, I will heal your daughter. Yes, I will do what you ask of me."

One reason I went into business instead of the ministry or social work was because of all the "yesses" that pile up in a minister's or social worker's life. Business seemed to offer a few more "nos." "No, I can't see you right now, I have an appointment." My friends used to joke that I would hire a taxi to take them home from the hospital if I had a board meeting or some other business meeting I could claim. Today, after listening to Lawreve's story, I say yes more often.

Just last night, for example, my next-door neighbor invited me to come over. I had just settled in for my favorite television program, my books scattered all around me to read during the commercials, when the phone rang. It was Betty, my eighty-four-year-old neighbor. "Laurie, could you bring your cat over? My granddaughter wants to see him." I knew Betty had been praying for three years that this granddaughter would come visit her. I winced. It was after 10 P.M., and this was the first time in nearly two weeks I could sit at home and relax. Maybe we could do it another time, I thought. Surely her granddaughter had seen cats before. Then I saw Lawreve in the background smiling and saying yes. I took a long deep breath. "Come on, Tomás," I said to the cat. "We've got a special person to go see." Is that what love is all about? Loving your next-door neighbor as much as you love yourself? "Yes," I could hear my heart laughing. Yes, yes, yes.

Jesus said yes.

Question

Experiment for twenty-four hours saying yes to others' requests.

Question

When have you spontaneously said yes to a request and been glad you did?

Question

Practice joyously, trustingly, happily saying yes more often. (The world has heard enough nos to last for a long, long time).

He Was
Open to People
and Their Ideas

One of the most powerful scenes in the film *Lawrence of Arabia* depicts the ten-day death march that Lawrence's army made through the desert. As the army staggered along, nearly dead from dehydration, they suddenly spied an oasis and eagerly fell into the water. When Lawrence took a head count, he noticed that one of the camel boys was missing. The boy's camel was found riderless near the back of the camp. Lawrence immediately told several of his men, "We must go back and find him." But the men refused to venture back into the merciless furnace of sand. "Master," they pleaded, "it is Allah's will that the boy did not return with us. His fate was written by God. We must not interfere."

Lawrence angrily remounted a camel and headed back into the dunes. The men stood there, shaking their heads. "Now we've lost him, too," they said as they returned to their rest. Two days later a shimmering image emerged from the heat wave. "It's Lawrence! He has found the boy!" the soldiers shouted as they ran forward to assist him. Lawrence leaned over and handed them the unconscious boy. He looked at their faces and said in a hoarse whisper, "Remember this: Nothing 'is written' unless you write it." Nothing is written unless you or I write it.

Why would a person with the authority and power of God go around asking people "What do you want me to do for you?" According to some religious doctrines, if Jesus really was the Son of God, he would not have asked people what they wanted — he would always be telling them what to do.

Not so. He constantly asked his staff members what they were thinking and asked the people in front of him, "What do you want?"

He encouraged people to ask for things and to be specific in their requests. "Ask and it shall be given to you. Knock on God's door and He'll open it."[70] "Would a son ask his father for bread and be given a stone? Or if he asks for fish, would he be given a serpent?"[71] The whole essence of the Bible is about a loving God trying to convince the children that he is eager to give them good things.

In the Garden of Eden, God the Creator brought the animals to Adam and Eve and said, "Whatever you call them, that will be their name."[72] Jesus said, "God always gives me what I ask of him."[73] In fact, there seems to be a divine yearning for a cooperative creative venture between God and humankind. God is looking for and is very interested in our ideas.

And if God is open to our ideas, shouldn't an Omega leader be open to her or his people and their ideas?

Life is about co-creation and companionship. What better way to demonstrate that than by being listening and responsive leaders?

Tom Peters, author, lecturer, and consultant, reveals that 75 percent of the most recent and innovative inventions came from people outside the profession. Apple Computers, for example, was born in a kid's garage — a kid who left the big boys because they would not listen to him.

Jesus was open to people and their ideas.

Question
When was the last time you listened to a staff member's idea?

Question

When was the last time you implemented a staff member's idea?

Question

Do you believe all the good ideas have to come from you?

He Empowered
Women

Unfortunately, women are not equally represented in leadership and managerial roles in organizations around the world, especially in churches and other companies that depend so much on their financial, spiritual, and physical contributions. Too many organizations still fail to recognize, acknowledge, or harness the energy and talents of women. Some still actively discourage and actually forbid women from taking leadership roles.

Jesus apparently felt differently. His first appearance after his death was to a woman, whose mission it was to go and convince the more doubtful males.[74] One man was so skeptical he had to plunge his fingers in

Jesus' wounds before *he* would believe.[75] God spoke first to a young Mary about a magnificent plan, which she was able to keep secret until the appropriate time. So, in the beginning and at the end of the gospel, God gave primary leadership roles to women. Mary literally conceived and helped deliver the message; wealthy women economically supported Jesus and his staff while they were on their mission;[76] and Mary Magdalene and Martha[77] were the first to recognize the miracle of the resurrection when it happened.[78] Although Jesus spent hours walking on the road to Emmaus with his male disciples after his resurrection, they did not recognize him.[79] Mary, however, recognized him almost instantly.

Several men have commented to me that they would promote more women if more women would come forward. Well, we are. Women currently own or operate 55 percent of the new businesses starting up. We ultimately control men's wealth because we outlive them. Women's ideas and methods are causing revolutions in countries, in companies, in churches, and in the professions we serve and are starting to lead.

Consider health care, for instance. Women are swelling the ranks of physicians. Currently, nearly 40 percent of all students in medical schools are female. In a recent survey the number one most requested attribute of a general physician was that she be a female. One local health care authority stated that most female physicians in San Diego have waiting lists.

Men who fail to acknowledge and enlist feminine energy often suffer for their arrogance. Pontius Pilate's wife, for example, tried to warn him not to be involved in the trial of Jesus. "I had a dream about him,"[80] she said. Pilate ignored her and signed Jesus' death warrant, and his own unenviable place in history.

Senator Paul Danforth's wife tried to warn him about the seriousness of Professor Anita Hill's allegations about Clarence Thomas. Senator Danforth, like the other males, tried to sweep the woman's complaint aside as being insignificant. The fiasco that ensued was caused primarily by men not taking women's concerns seriously.

One comedienne theorized that perhaps the reason the Israelites wandered in the wilderness for forty years was because Moses wouldn't give Miriam the map.

Jesus said to both women and men, "The kingdom is within you."[81] He delegated equal power and authority to anyone who asked. He said in heaven there is neither male nor female, and he came to see that things were done "on earth, as it is in heaven."[82] On the television show *Star Trek: The Next Generation*, Captain Picard never went into new territory without the intuitive female counselor, Troi, at his side. Often she was sent in ahead of everybody else to assess the situation.

So, men, make way for the women. Recruit them,

and you will be the wiser. Women, we must claim and own our power. After all, how far can men really go without us? Only one generation.

Jesus empowered women.

Question

What percentage of top *leadership roles* are held by women in your organization, company, or church?

Question

How does this compare with its population; that is, how many women *work or serve* in your organization, company, or church?

Question

If the percentage seems unrepresentative, what are you willing to do about it, and why?

He Was
Transparent
Before Them

According to the Scriptures, Jesus appeared between the ghosts of Elijah and Moses on the Mount of Transfiguration. The verse recounts, "And Jesus became transfigured (or transparent) before them."[83]

This scene is not only about magical heavenly essences; it also illustrates an important principle. Jesus was transparent because he had nothing to hide. He had no hidden agenda. He had no secret pockets.

Covering up some aspect of a situation implies "I'm greater than you." Although the objective may be to protect, it is ultimately patronizing. This kind of attitude breeds resentment and retaliation. During the Iran-Contra scandal, the prosecutors focused not so much on what was done but on the fact that the perpetrators had lied about it. "He who covers a matter gets punished. He who confesses a matter receives mercy."[84]

As a leader, you should not cloister yourself in an ivory tower thinking you have facts that your staff is not prepared to handle . . . not just facts about the company, but also facts about yourself. Barbara Bush talked about her wrinkles freely, and the public adored her. We all have wrinkles we're trying to cover up with pearls. Sharing some personal facts about ourselves makes us more like others. The more we are viewed as being like others, the more others actually like us.

Many people have detailed the power of mimicry to establish a bond between strangers. Simply by adopting similar postures and expressions, people begin to identify with you — no matter what your differences in attitude and philosophy are. Peer pressure is predicated on mimicry. We all look for signs that we are not alone . . . that, in fact, we are like others.

The Phantom of the Opera is a classic example of how *not* to motivate others. Wanting love, the Phantom subverts his true talents, dons a mask, and lives in the underworld, trying to motivate people through tricks, loud organ music, smoke, and other negative special effects. The end result is that people fear him and hunt him down. Only when the mask is ripped off does he receive an honest, sincere kiss from the lovely Christine.

Do you operate like the Phantom, using half masks, closed doors, and whispers in smoke-filled rooms? Or is your leadership style more transparent? People can handle the truth. In fact, they probably sense it already. When you are totally open with them, true love and learning begin.

Jesus did not hide his tears or his fears. He was transparent before his people.

Question

What fact or situation are you trying to keep from your staff?

Question

What are the obstacles that keep you from being a transparent leader?

He Believed
in Them

J esus looked at the earnest young man and said, "Some people say your name is Simon. But I am going to call you Peter. And upon this rock I will build my church."[85] Simon meant "the Flaky One," while Peter meant "the Rock." Surely Jesus must have seen something special in Peter, because his record shows that he was a rather impetuous guy—hardly the kind of person you would declare to be the foundation of everything you were doing.

Peter pulled such stunts as trying to keep Jesus from going to Jerusalem because he was afraid, cutting off the Roman guard's ear with a sword after Jesus had preached love and forgiveness to him for three years, and ultimately denying even knowing Jesus when Jesus was sent to prison. Jesus knew this man intimately, and yet he called him "my rock."

Jesus had to believe in his staff or he never would have slept nights. Their backgrounds were not glorious, and they did not grasp what he was saying most of the time. They were constantly arguing over who would get to sit where in the kingdom, and they dozed off and forgot him when he needed them most. Yet these were the people he chose to work with, and he visualized the best in each of them, even when there was evidence to the contrary. He poured a mold of greatness for them to fill, and ultimately they went on to fill it.

Perhaps it was this inner knowledge that allowed Jesus to give his staff authority. He freely shared with them his longings, his heartaches, and his fears. If he did not believe in them, he would not have called them brothers and sisters. He would not have taken them home with him.

People tend to rise to the occasion when they have someone who truly believes in them. Perhaps we just need someone to show us who we really are inside. Perhaps that is what we are all so desperately searching for — someone to acknowledge the goodness that we each sense about ourselves but are so hesitant to share.

Peter went on to preach the good news of equal access to God to the formerly shunned Gentiles.[86] No other preacher or prophet had been called to go to the "unclean" Gentiles before with such good news. Peter eventually was crucified for his controversial work. In deference to Jesus, it is said, he asked to be crucified upside down. This request came from a man whom everyone but Jesus called "the Flaky One."

To have someone we admire believe in us can help set our greatness free. It certainly worked for Peter.

Jesus believed in his staff.

Question

Write down any new insights you might have now about the ones you might have been writing off, like Peter, as "flaky."

Question

How can you show your staff members you believe in them?

He Clearly
Defined Their
Work-Related Benefits

One of my financial planner friends stated, "Jesus offered his staff one heck of a 401-K retirement plan." In fact, Jesus was constantly advising his staff on ways to identify and increase their true wealth. He also said, "I came that they might have life, and have it *abundantly*."[87] Jesus' definition of wealth might not be the same as ours, but he clearly defined the rewards to people who worked with him.

People are more willing to give up something if they can attain something else of greater perceived value. The man who sold everything he had in order to purchase "the pearl of great price" *got* "the pearl of great price."[88] Leaders who think others will follow them for no reason, because it is their job description, or because they are afraid to do otherwise, fail to understand a key element of the human psyche. People will give up what they are used to only when they clearly understand and are shown something better. The trick is understanding and communicating the difference between good and better.

Many times leaders and managers expect their employees to leap through the flames for them but do not define what the purpose or reward will be. Then they wonder why nobody is leaping. One of my favorite Gary Larson cartoons shows a trainer holding a flaming hoop in front of a turtle, saying "Jump, Mortimer, jump!" This clearly shows a case of ineffective and meaningless communication.

Another Larson cartoon shows a man talking to a dog named Ginger, issuing all sorts of commands. The cartoon shows what the dog is hearing: "blah blah blah Ginger . . . blah blah blah Ginger." In other words, the dog is hearing only its name in everything the master is saying. That illustrates human nature, too. As Harry Pickens, a marketing seminar leader, said, "People are constantly tuned in to one station: WIFM. And those call letters stand for "What's in It for Me?"

Jesus clearly defined his staff's work-related benefits.

Question

Define your employees' work-related benefits.

Question

Which benefits go beyond purely financial re-wards?

Question

List three things per month that you could do to make your employees' lives more abundant.

He Forgave Them

Forgiveness is like oil in an engine. It keeps the wheels moving. Forgiveness is like gravity . . . invisible in its power yet profound in its effects. Jesus is the ultimate symbol of forgiveness. He kept on believing in his staff. He kept on giving them chances.

Jesus had a true sense of "try, try again." He always gave people another chance. Tom Peters says corporations should actually reward people for failure, because failure means risk; and without risk there can be no success. If your employees are afraid to make mistakes, they will be afraid to make much of anything.

I was once in a self-discovery group where people

were not mincing words. One man, sitting very stiffly and quietly, was a candidate for promotion within his organization. His body language was a picture of caution and fear. Finally, a woman gave him this sound advice: "You just need to fail a few times. Then you will understand that people are going to love you even when you are not perfect."

A forgiving attitude creates forward motion. I encountered this recently when my business partner made a decision for the company without my knowing about it. I was upset because it directly affected seven other people. My first reaction was anger. I challenged her action. She immediately responded defensively. Since we were at a client conference, we especially needed to remain a team, so we both backed off a little and approached the problem from one another's shoes. "What were you thinking when you made that decision?" I asked her, knowing that she had only everyone's best interest at heart. She explained and then asked me why I was so angry. I explained my rationale. We both repeated word for word one another's reasoning. Then we decided on a formula for action that would meet both our needs in the future. Within a few minutes we were able to emerge from our discussion as a team again. (As it turned out, her instincts were right.)

Forgiveness does not mean being a doormat or not using discretion in whom you deal with and how. Forgiveness means allowing others to make mistakes while you and they keep moving forward.

Peter, the one who pledged eternal faithfulness to Jesus, denied him three times publicly.[89] It must have been difficult for Jesus to forgive, yet he appeared to Peter and forgave him, asking him to show his love now by "feeding his sheep."[90]

Sometimes, as with Peter, the farther they fall, the deeper they will love.

Jesus forgave them.

Q u e s t i o n
What situations have you had to forgive lately?

Q u e s t i o n
Who has forgiven you in memorable ways?

Q u e s t i o n
What is your feeling toward them now?

He Treated
Them as Equals

The ancient Hebrews were hesitant to even utter the name of God.[91] In the Old Testament a soldier was once struck dead because he touched the Ark of the Covenant while unclean (and not a Levite).[92]

Ancient Levitical law decreed that people with physical deformities were not allowed to enter the Temple.[93] In the Old Testament God was portrayed as being extremely strict. Scripture after Scripture said that God was so pure he could not even look at evil, much less tolerate it. The entire religious system was based on teaching people how to become pure enough to enter his presence (and thereby avoid getting struck by lightning).

When Jesus arrived on the historical scene, most people were still considered to be impure — some because of their deeds, some because of their race (for instance, the Gentiles). Women were impure at least once a month.[94] Anyone was impure if he or she ate pork. In other words, only a precious few were pure enough even to approach God. Only Moses could talk directly to him,[95] and even he had to shield his face.

Jesus declared himself to be related to God yet mingled with prostitutes, thieves, and tax collectors. You can imagine how this upset the religious hierarchy. Not only God's identity, but their identity (and power base) was being threatened.

Jesus, representing God, treated everyone as his equal. He could move mountains, raise the dead, heal the sick, and make the lame walk and the blind see. Yet he called fishermen and prostitutes his brothers and sisters. He not only accepted these "less-than-pure" individuals, he radiated so much love for them that people swarmed to him. People felt good about themselves in his presence.

During my three-year stint working at a women's resource center, I was able to view two very contrasting leadership styles. Catherine, who founded the center, embodied the Omega leadership style. She treated secretaries and volunteers with the same warmth and respect that she did members of the board. When she needed something typed, she would ask the secretary up front if she had the time to do it. Then she was truly grateful for the work when it was finished. "This is a work of art," she would declare, and the secretary would leave just beaming. Catherine knew the names of everyone in each staff member's family, and she took the time to inquire about each one of them on her way in.

The leader who took her place, however, had a different management style. She immediately began to close her office door and communicate through memos. She knew nothing of her employees' family situations, nor did she inquire. She barked orders as if everything were due her. When it came to lunch hour, nobody wanted to go out with her. When extra projects came in, she had to demand that people stay overtime. Nobody wanted to be around her because of her superior air. Productivity at the center plummeted, because staff members had been used to being treated as equals.

Jesus showed respect by meeting people where they were and accepting them for who they were. In the light of this acceptance, people wanted to be better, try harder, and do the good and right thing. His respect empowered them.

He treated them as equals.

Question

Is your management style based on equality or hierarchies?

Question

Do people feel good about themselves in your presence?

He Educated Them

One sentence sums up the focus of Jesus' time on earth: "And he went everywhere teaching, healing and preaching."[96] Since teaching is educating the mind and preaching is educating the heart, two-thirds of Jesus' work was education.

If you look at the instances when he healed people, nine times out of ten he spoke to them about an attitude change or a new way of behaving that was to go along with their physical state of being. "Go, and sin no more."[97] I feel safe in saying education was Jesus' number-one priority.

Someone recently told me that professors on the whole live longer than any other professional group. One theory for this is that they keep stretching their minds and tend to immerse themselves in mentally stimulating atmospheres long after retirement.

Yet most corporations, in a crunch, cut back on training programs. It happens every time. We will fund tin and metal before we will fund the human mind. Our country spends far more money on defense than on education, and our teachers are still among our lowest-paid professionals. As a former vice president so aptly misstated, "A mind is a terrible thing not to have."

In the wonderful book *Do It!*, authors John Roger and Peter McWilliams assert that human beings are built for success but programmed for failure. Jesus' mission was to deliver our crown, and he knew we needed a new mind and heart in order for us to be able to receive it.

He educated people.

Question

How much time do you spend educating your employees?

Question

What kind of formal training programs are in place?

Question

What are *you* currently learning that's new?

He Managed
from the
Inside Out

Have you ever noticed that many times the grass immediately surrounding a sprinkler head is brown? I call this the *Sprinkler Phenomenon of Management*. So much energy and drive is going to the outer reaches of the yard that the grass closest to the source of the water is left dry.

We often overlook the people closest to us, despite our good intentions. Many times receptionists at large corporations are unaware that a major event is being held in the building. Preachers' kids are notorious for their own lack of shepherding.

I recently did a series of seminars at an osteopathic

hospital in Texas where 75 percent of the staff did not know what the term *osteopathic* meant. This hospital had spent nearly $500,000 educating the public through television and newspaper ads, yet the cooks, the clerks, the cleaning crew, and the admitting staff still did not know what *osteopathic* meant. The administration hired me to help correct that problem.

After one of my seminars, a security guard who had worked at the hospital for fifteen years expressed his excitement at finally knowing the hospital's mission. He said, "People used to ask me what *osteopathic* meant, and I had to tell them I didn't know. Now I do. Can I have some more of those flyers please? I want to pass them out to my friends."

You may think: So what if the security guard knows more about the hospital's mission? What will the difference be to the bottom line? Plenty. Everyone rules an empire . . . even if it is one we might not care to inhabit. As your people communicate with their people, your company's influence and reputation will grow.

Jesus understood the theory of educating and informing his people first. He practiced the "ripple" style of management, depending on small circles to spread into bigger ones. A good public relations plan will include both internal and external PR. If I had to choose one over the other, I would choose internal PR as my top priority.

As a public relations and marketing consultant for a

STRENGTH OF RELATIONSHIPS

number of physicians and hospitals, I always remind the physicians that their staff can make them or break them. A recent study presented the top seven reasons patients left their doctors. Number one, of course, was inability to get along with or trust the physician. Number two was inability to get along with or trust the physician's staff. (Number five was outdated magazines in the waiting room, and number seven was disputes over billing.) This study shows that if patients do not like the receptionist, they may leave and never tell the doctor why. I have become so adamant about the importance of the ripple effect that if a physician does not include her or his staff in the planning process, I will not work with that client.

An Omega physician also takes the time to train staff members as to the discomforts involved in the procedures they perform. This training makes them more sympathetic and understanding of their clients — the patients.

Jesus looked at the crowd and said, "Phillip, how shall we feed all these people?"[98] Phillip's practical suggestion was to send them home so they could find their own dinner. But Jesus was concerned, because he knew they would faint along the way. He enlisted Phillip's help in solving their hunger. He taught Phillip to empathize with people the way he did.

He made sure his staff knew what was going on at all times. He kept the grass closest to him green.

Jesus managed from the inside out.

Question

Do you sometimes overlook the people closest to you? If so, what can you do to correct that?

Question

What is your system for making sure your staff is constantly informed about the facts as well as the emotions or spirit of a situation?

He Held Them
Accountable

❧

Accountability is a key factor in management because it is the cornerstone of empowerment and personal growth. If no one is accountable for a project, no one gets to grow through the experience of it.

Accountability has nothing to do with blame. It has everything to do with individual and corporate growth. Accomplished tasks breed self-confidence. Self-confidence breeds success. And success breeds more success. The rich get richer and the poor get poorer.

A young physician I know says most of her patients are shocked when she completes her diagnosis and meets them in her office with "These are the test results. These are your options. Which do you choose?" She says they still expect her to tell them what to do. She explains to them gently and firmly that it is their health, their life, their choice.

Holding people accountable allows them the opportunity to sign their name on a portrait of success, no matter how small that portrait might be. It gives them their next growth challenge in a defined and measurable form. To treat them as equals is to hold them accountable.

When groups show via corporate culture — which is decided at the top — that accountability is to be worn like a medal, rather than an albatross, people will be more eager to wear it around their necks.

Jesus said, "Whatever you ask for, will be done. Whatever you loose on earth, will be loosed in heaven. Whatever you bind up, will be bound."[99]

Jesus held people accountable.

Question
Do you constantly rescue others, or do you hold them accountable?

Question
How do you do both?

He Spent
Lots of Time
with Them

We humans have a tremendous need for companionship. Jesus knew about this need, and he fulfilled it. Even when he was leaving, his words were not "Okay, remember points one, two, and three," or "Peter, keep your eyes on the horizon when walking on water." His words to them were "Don't cry. I will be *with you* always."[100]

Companionship is a very precious and expensive commodity because it can be bought only with the one thing that seems to be so scarce: time. Georgia O'Keeffe wrote in a letter to a friend, "To see a flower takes time, just like to have a friend takes time."

Catherine, who started out as my boss, has become one of my most cherished friends. I will always be grateful for her guidance throughout my career, but what I treasure most is some of our "meaningless conversations." She once took the time to describe in detail a dress she saw in New York that would highlight the color of my eyes. She regaled me one morning with her story about how she was late to work because her son Brian's chicks had hatched in the garage and she couldn't start the car until she caught all thirty-six of them. She called me one lazy Saturday and described how her husband Edgar calls the cat, "Come here, Monstie, come here," puckering his lips just so, and yet Monstie always bites him anyway. We laughed and laughed. Meaningless conversations, really.

Yet even though I've long had access to her substantial library, the book I most often flip through is my mental scrapbook . . . of our long walks on the Rio Grande or us sitting by the pool sipping Pepsis and planning our destinies. She says the mission statement for our friendship is "to love, support, and challenge each other to fully live our dreams."

I've called her when I didn't know who else to call, and she's called me after key board meetings just to see how things went. In fact, Catherine has invested thousands of hours in me over the past fourteen or fifteen years. That is why now, many years after working for her, I would do anything in my power to make her world somehow better. She is a leader who spent lots of time with me.

During the war in the Persian Gulf, General Norman Schwarzkopf spent lots of time with the press. He spent lots of time with his troops, too. This is the kind of leadership that the world hungers for. Not the distant, wave-from-the-balcony leadership that "royalty" demonstrates.

Jesus spent lots of time with his staff.

And I wonder whether it wasn't really the picnics and the echoes of his laughter that bound their hearts to him so. Because ultimately they moved heaven and earth just to *be with* him again. In his last recorded memo on earth (John 17), Jesus requested five different times that he and his staff be "one" again. That theme of oneness came through right before he died, because perhaps Jesus' real mission was about companionship.

The Omega leader takes the time to be with his or her staff: on picnics, carefully planned retreats, long walks by the river. At hospitals, funerals, weddings, birthdays, and all the insignificant days in between. This is where, when, and how people learn what love is. And when people learn that they are loved, they will follow that leader anywhere.

Jesus spent lots of time with his staff.

Question

How much quality time do you spend with your people?

Question

Is your time with them always structured?

Question

Do you check on your staff to see how they are *really* doing, or do you call only when you want something?

He Touched
the Fragile Things

Willy, a talented artist, potter, and friend of mine, recently had her first art show. Friends and family were invited to the preopening reception. Willy's five-year-old godchild, Megan, was led carefully through the gallery while her mother pointed out each piece, telling her not to touch anything that might break. At the end of the day, Willy asked Megan, "What do you like best of all the things you see here?" Megan leaned forward and whispered, "I want to touch the fragile things."

Late that night I got a phone call from my mother. "Honey, Grandmother passed away tonight." We'd all been expecting it. She was ninety-one years old. But just the day before, she had been correcting my grammar and teasing the nurses saying, "It sure is hard to be a princess around here." And I sat on the bed with tears in my eyes and thought "Life is so very frail. *I* want to touch the fragile things."

We all want to touch "the fragile things," but so few of us take the time to do so. Many times we fail to recognize fragile things when we see them.

Jesus took the time to touch the fragile things. He took the time to play with the children. He took the time to notice the lilies, swaying fragrantly in the field. He took the time to notice a baby sparrow that had fallen to the ground. He took the time to notice the number of fine gray hairs on an old man's head. He took the time to hold the hands of a little girl and time to weep with a grieving family.

Most of life is centered on attaining fragile things, but we often lose sight of their true meaning and begin to sacrifice ourselves to the process of acquiring them or their substitutes.

An art exhibit at the Museum of Contemporary Art in La Jolla recently featured the work of an artist who had photographed diamond mine workers deep in South Africa. I found it ironic that the jeweler next door to the museum seized upon this marketing opportunity by displaying with great fanfare and steep prices *his* glittering jewels. The photographer had focused on one of the struggling mine workers who had wrapped a purple towel around his glistening forehead. He photographed beads of sweat running down the worker's trembling legs, straining under the burden of rocks that were too heavy. The photographer zeroed in on a scraped knuckle that had been left unattended in the rush to carry out the diamond-bearing ore. The artist was showing us the true "fragile things." Yet these were not the things we could wear on our fingers.

Jesus warned about a generation that was always out looking for signs but missing the breezes. He told us about a place and time where all tears would be wiped away. Where the lion would lie down with the lamb. Where everyone would know and appreciate the fragile things. But the machines of humanity just kept on going . . . the power machines, the hunger machines, the let's-get-back-to-the-rules machines, the let's-talk-bottom-line machines. The status quo.

Any worthwhile leader will have a respect for those types of machines and the thoughts that fuel them. But she or he must remember, always, to seek and touch the fragile things. We cannot live by bread alone.

Jesus touched the fragile things.

Question
List some of the "fragile things" in your life.

Question

Describe some of the "fragile things" in your employees' lives. What do they hold most dear?

Question

How do you help them to hold and keep and nourish their "fragile things"?

He Set
an Example
for Them

There is a popular saying that children learn by what they see, not by what they hear. Policy manuals and instruction books may serve a purpose, but they do not establish a corporate culture. Leaders set the example by what they do.

When Jesus took his garment off and used it as a towel to wash the staffers' feet, they were shocked and protested that they should be washing his feet. He said, "I am doing this to set an example for you."[101] Nothing he said could have had as much power as watching him do this most humble deed.

I was at a restaurant with some friends one night when we saw a father and his two sons walk in. The father was a handsome man with dark hair and a mustache, dressed in finely tailored clothes. He obviously had something on his mind because his brow was furrowed and his hands were stuck deep in his pockets as he walked, eyes straight ahead. His sons, who looked maybe six and eight years old, followed two steps behind him. Dark-haired like their daddy, they, too, had their hands stuck deep in their pockets and were striding forward with a serious glare. Their expression, their stride, their posture, and their intent were mirror images of their father. Unfortunately, he was too self-absorbed to notice their unconscious imitation of him. Everyone in the restaurant noticed, however, as heads turned and people smiled.

When a leader arrives late but demands punctuality, the cognitive dissonance that is created will manifest itself in various ways in the staff members' attitudes. Corporate culture is established at the top by one or two key individuals. A bit of red dye injected into a potato soon has every inch of the potato showing red in its veins. Your deeds and behaviors will be injected like dye into the psyche of your staff members. I hope you like red potatoes, because you'll soon be eating your deeds.

Jesus set an example for his staff.

Question

Would you be willing to have someone videotape your deeds for a day and then use that tape as a training video?

Question

What kind of "by-example" training is your staff now receiving?

He Prayed
for Them

In the Old Testament the Levites were the tribe designated to be priests for the Israelites, and they were given a very distinctive wardrobe to wear.[102] Their breastplates, or *ephods*, consisted of specially carved stones with each of the twelve tribes' names inscribed on them. This was done so that the Levite priests would literally have the tribes of Israel upon their hearts night and day. Elsewhere in the Old Testament God is said to love his people so much that he has inscribed each person's name in the palm of his hand.[103]

Jesus described a loving God so attentive to each of his children that he knows how many inches tall they are and even how many hairs they each have on their heads.[104] Prayer means not only asking for heavenly intercession but also being in an ongoing contemplative, meditative state on behalf of each loved one.

I know a highly successful executive who lights a candle for each of her clients even though she is not Catholic. She says she likes the ritual and the visual reminder of each client. Often while in this state of meditation and prayer she receives wonderful ideas on their behalf.

Imagine what kind of management this nation would have if CEOs spent as much time mulling and praying over their staffers' growth as they did over their budget reports. This would give new meaning to the term *a closely held corporation*. Leaders and managers often spend too much energy trying to make numbers dance. Anyone can tell you that numbers don't dance. Only people do.

Jesus prayed for people.

Q u e s t i o n

How often do you contemplate each member of your staff in a prayerful, meditative way?

Q u e s t i o n

What significant difference has prayer made in the progress of your business affairs, especially regarding your staff's needs and concerns?

He Acknowledged
Them in Public
and in Private

The National Retailers Association recently asked retail workers to list in order of importance their reasons for working. The number-one reason was "Appreciation by others for what I do." The number-two reason was "Respect." The number-three reason was "Money." These results might surprise some people. However, most of us realize that today people no longer have to accept just any job and be grateful for it. Money is not the primary reason we work. The benefits we really are seeking are appreciation and respect.

Jesus constantly praised his staff members and told them "Well done." In many of his stories he spoke of masters praising faithful workers. God himself opened up the heavens and praised Jesus in public, once at the river, saying "This is my beloved son, in whom I am well pleased,"[105] and once on the mountain, saying "This is my beloved son. Hear him."[106] (Even God knows how important public acknowledgment is to motivate and keep good people.)

We never outgrow the need for someone to appreciate what we are doing. At the driving range you will see many well-dressed middle-age and older men seriously whacking at the ball. They then turn around to see if anyone noticed how far it went. In work and in play, at every age, we need to be acknowledged.

A friend of mine once was assigned a difficult project and given a short deadline in which to accomplish it. Although she was paid well for her work, at one point she almost quit, saying in frustration "Bill never tells me whether it's good or not! I wish he would give me some feedback!" She communicated this in exasperation one day to Bill's partner, who explained, "Susan you will never get any positive feedback from Bill. He was an outstanding athlete in high school and college, went on to become a multimillionaire at a very early age, and still never heard a positive or approving word from his father. Unfortunately, this has carried over into his work. You'll just have to trust in yourself to know when it is good or not." This explanation helped her understand Bill a little more, but she was still missing a key element of satisfaction in her work.

Susan learned to get feedback from her friends. One night at a dinner party she proudly showed each perfect page of her project to her appreciative and communicative friends. Bill soon discovered what a mistake he had made by not praising Susan. As a result of her dinner meeting, Susan got another and better offer for a similar project from one of the admiring dinner guests.

Everyone needs positive feedback. If you want to watch someone grow several inches in stature before your eyes, just praise her or him in public.

Once on a three-hour layover in Chicago, I visited a small pub near the airport. It was freezing weather, and the pub was so cold that the piano player was playing with gloves on. I sat next to her and was amazed at how beautifully she played. I had never heard such lovely piano music, much less when the pianist was playing with gloved hands. I asked her if she would make a special tape for me of some of the songs she was playing. I wanted to give it to a friend of mine who loves music. The pianist sat up even taller and straighter after that, and she played her heart out. As I was leaving, I gave her my business card and some advance money for the tape. Then I called the owner of the pub and said, "I've asked Dorothy to make a tape of all these songs she's playing. If she made copies available here, would you promote them? I think your patrons would love to take a part of the pub's special atmosphere home with them. Dorothy is really one of the best piano players I have ever heard." The owner enthusiastically agreed to help promote Dorothy's tape once it was completed. Dorothy was in her late fifties, and I learned from one of the patrons that her husband was dying of cancer. She played the piano at night to help pay for his medical bills.

Four weeks later I got a two-hour custom tape of the music I loved, along with a note from Dorothy. She told me how much my acknowledgment of her gift meant. Six weeks later I got an invitation and an announcement. She was performing her first concert for the public . . . for pay, in a concert hall. She might have gone on to the next level of performance anyway, but I still wonder if perhaps my simple five minutes of praise was the final push she needed to acknowledge and expand her own gift.

In the 1980s Nordstrom Department Stores became famous for the way they acknowledged their staff. The daughter of a friend of mine who worked there won the top sales award for her department. One day, as she was working, the entire Nordstrom management team gathered around her and told her one by one how much they valued the way she was representing Nordstrom's to the customers. Then they handed here a crisp $100 bill. This was done in the middle of the day, in front of her coworkers and customers. She loved her job, and part of the reason was that she got paid with more than money from her bosses.

Jesus acknowledged his team members in public and in private.

Question

Describe the last time you publicly praised one of your staff.

Question

If public words of praise were your staff's only paycheck, how much would they be making?

Question

What are some tangible acknowledgments you could develop and give to your staff?

He Looked Out
for the Little Guys

❧

"Zacchaeus, come down from that tree. I want to have dinner at your house tonight."[107] This request gave Zacchaeus a tremendous boost in public stature. He was a man who was so short, he had to climb up in a tree to see Jesus.

Jesus recognized people's insecurities and rushed to reassure them. "Simon," he said, "they call you a flake but I call you the Rock." Another time he said, "Mary Magdalene, they say you are worthy of death but I say you are worthy of life." And yet another time: "Do not push the children back. They should be at the center. In fact, if you want to enter heaven you must become one of them."[108] I sometimes wonder if Jesus wasn't given a choice of transportation into Jerusalem. Elijah got white horses, but maybe Jesus thought the donkey could use a little boost to its self-esteem.

Jesus was always looking out for and protecting the little ones. King David changed a long-held tradition when he insisted that the ones who stayed behind and guarded the baggage get an equal share of the spoils of conquest. David believed that "they also serve, who only stand and wait."

Jesus took the time to see the people in the shadows. The wallflowers. The lepers. The ones nobody wanted to dance with. He asked them to dance. Jesus dined with the elite, but he lived with the little guys . . . the common folks, the fishermen.

Perhaps Jesus was sensitive to the unlovely and unloved because he knew what it was like to be considered an outsider. He knew what it felt like to be spit at, mislabeled, and verbally and physically abused. He knew how it felt to be treated like a king one day and a criminal the next.

When he looked at little Zacchaeus in the tree, he said, "Come stand on equal ground with me. I'd consider it an honor to dine at your house tonight."

The rich people may have buried Jesus, but the common folks gave him life and joy and companionship.

Jesus looked out for the little guys.

STRENGTH OF RELATIONSHIPS

Question

Do you spend time with the little guys in your organization, or do you constantly position your time and energy with the big guys?

Question

Describe a few of the times you have taken the time to acknowledge the people around you . . . the ones who serve silently and with little recognition.

Question

How do you use your position to help make your staff feel wonderful, more valued, and encouraged?

He Enrolled Them

⟨⟨⟩⟩

Jesus not only inspired others, he enrolled them. He not only excited people, he got them to sign up. He asked his staff out loud and often, "Will you follow me?" When he became more controversial, a number of his followers decided to leave. Jesus turned to Peter and said, "Are you, too, going to leave?" Peter replied, "You have the words of life. Where else would I go?"[109] Yet Jesus did ask the question.

It is easy to make a sales presentation but not have the courage to ask for the order. Jesus always asked for the order. He enrolled his team. He asked them publicly for a verbal contract. "I will do these things. Will you be on my team?" Then he waited for the answer.

Many times leaders get so excited communicating a need to the crowd that they leave without signing anyone up to help solve it. Leaders are responsible for clearly communicating the work-related benefits to their staff, and the staff is responsible for clearly communicating its commitment to the leader. However, the burden of asking the question and getting people to sign up falls on the leader. Perhaps some leaders do not ask the commitment question because they are afraid of the answer.

Jesus did not proceed with his working relationships until he knew where each person stood. Like all good leaders, he was looking for commitment from his staff. He deserved it, as does anyone who is willing to stand up for a cause.

In our advertising agency, The Jones Group, before we take final artwork to the printer, we require clients to sign off on the project. Their signatures declare that the artwork is correct. You would be amazed at how tiny some people's signatures suddenly become. Whereas before they used flamboyant capital letters that took up half a page, suddenly their signatures shrink to illegible scratchings. Sometimes they even ask if they can sign in pencil. We always smile and hand them a pen.

John Hancock, whose name has become synonymous with the word *signature*, has the largest signature on the Declaration of Independence. It is said that after he signed it, he turned to his comrades and said, "I don't want the king to have any problem finding my name." That is courage and commitment with a capital C. John Hancock was enrolled in the mission.

One of the key negotiating skills is the ability to ask a question and then fall totally silent as you await the response. This is particularly effective with hard questions. People are uncomfortable with silence and will rush to fill it, often to their own disadvantage.

Jesus asked, "Will you follow me?" and then waited for the answer. He asked Peter, "Do you love me?" and then waited for the answer. He asked, "Will you wait in the garden with me?"[110] and then waited for the answer.

Jesus enrolled people.

Question

When did you last ask your staff members what their commitment to you and the project is?

Question

Do you wait for the answer after you have asked a hard question?

Question

What kind of commitment do you expect from your staffers—verbal or otherwise—before they can be considered part of the team?

He Kept
Urging Them On

Jesus kept urging people on. "You can do it. Take up your bed and walk. Come on, Lazarus. Come into the light. Come on, Peter. Step out on the water. Come on!"

One of the saddest stories in the Scriptures is about the tribes that chose to settle in the desert before reaching the promised land. They got what they asked for, but all they asked for was sand.[111] When Jesus turned water into wine, he was saying "You are divine. Every day can be a feast for you when you know that you are loved."

Some lyrics for a song I wrote are:

Song of the Desert

If you go out to the desert
listen closely to the sound.
You will hear the breezes sighing
to the silent cactus clustered round.

Why are you here? You know where you could be.

But that would have meant replanting.
A cold winter.
Surely death —

Giving up our ounce of water
For some distant, far-off, promised spring.

But he told you that if you'd believe, that you would see.

"Go away . . . we're happy here."
The owl hooted, "Go away.
At least here we have our shadows."
The snake smiled . . . curled up in the sand.

How frustrating it must have been for Jesus to see the people he said were gods acting like mindless lumps of clay. We don't ask for too much; we ask for too little.

Jesus kept urging people on.

Question

In what ways do you encourage your people to try harder, do more, and be the best they can be?

Question

From whom do you receive *your* encouragement?

He Had Compassion
for the Crowds

Jesus desperately wanted to show people how loved they were. "Oh, Jerusalem. How often I would have gathered you under my wings," he cried.[112] When he saw a city in spiritual shambles, he literally cried from the anguish. Sometimes the wasted energy, the empty seats at the banquet, and all the pain and loneliness overcame him. Jesus wept.[113]

Jesus personally felt other people's pain. I remember being very sick one time and a friend saying "I wish I could absorb your pain so that it would go away and leave you alone." That is compassion . . . and empathy.

My mother, who is an advocate for AIDS victims,

once told me that when she told God she would help him, she had no idea it meant walking in other people's shoes. "They're not ever my size." She laughed. Sometimes she does laundry for the AIDS patients. One night she sat and sang lullabies in Spanish to a young man named Eduardo as he lay dying.

As Jesus turned to face the crowded church, he asked, "And who is godly here? Who has the courage? Who has compassion? Who deserves the crown? The one who wears the white robe and rinses his hands after passing out crackers intoning to the crowds that others are dying a justified death . . . or the woman who sits by the side of a dying man, or comforting a child she knows will also soon die of AIDS?"

I, too, sometimes look at churches and weep. For once we lose our compassion, we lose our souls. When the heart stops beating, the whole body dies.

Suppose that you are the captain of a huge aircraft carrier out in the South China Sea. Your crewmen suddenly alert you that a plane is approaching. The message says that it is South Vietnamese, and it is running out of fuel. The plane must land on your deck or perish in the sea. The pilot says aboard are himself, his wife, and their five children. They are escaping from North Vietnam. There is only one small problem. There is no room on the deck for them and no time to move the other planes. What would you do?

In this situation, the captain pushed three multi-million-dollar aircraft into the sea. He was an Omega leader. He listened to his heart. How much is a human life worth to you?

Jesus had compassion for the crowds.

Question

List three examples of compassionate leadership that you have observed recently.

Question

When have you displayed compassion as a leader?

He Served Them

The principle of service is what separates true leaders from glory seekers. Jesus, the leader, served his people. Most religions teach that we are put here to serve God; yet, in Jesus, God is offering to serve us.

Picture the shift in thinking. Old Testament mentality looked at humanity as being indebted to God, trying to find countless ways to please Him. Then along comes a man claiming to be the very son of God, who asks people, "What would you like me to do for you?"

Some people are shocked at the inference that God serves us. Yet this man who represented God — who was imbued with all the power of God — walked up to people and asked, "How can I help you?" If they wanted to see, he opened their eyes. If they wanted to walk, he let them walk. If they wanted a daughter brought back to life, he brought their daughter back to life. If they wanted wine, he gave them wine. If they wanted bread, he gave them bread. Even when they wanted him dead, he died. He did all of these things without a fight, all because he was coming from one power: love. To love is to serve. And God is love.

The symbol of love is a circle. True service inspires service, which completes the circle. That might be why we get so upset when we are not served and why we are willing to pay more to a person who offers to serve us. Subconsciously he or she is are saying "I'm part of the circle with you."

The true attitude of service is a softening agent that works on the hardest of hearts and situations. I witnessed this when I visited Beau, one of my high school friends in Dallas. He had to deliver fifteen huge custom pillows he had made to the fourth floor of the Dallas Trade Center. It was winter, and the wind was blowing and it was spitting rain. The client had told Beau to park in the back and just run the pillows up to her, so he dutifully parked in a yellow service zone and proceeded to unload the car. Sure enough, a security guard hurried over and barked, "Hey, you can't park there!" My defenses went up. I started to reply with some authority that Ms. Higgins — who probably signed his paycheck — had given us permission. I was not too happy about the prospect of parking half a mile away and lugging fifteen huge pillows in the rain. Beau, however, proceeded to demonstrate why he had won the highest service award bestowed by our high school. He put down the pillows and said with the utmost sincerity, "Ms. Higgins told me that I could park here for just a few minutes, but maybe I made a mistake. You're the boss. Tell me exactly what you want me to do and I'll do it." He looked the security guard in the eyes and smiled.

I had never seen such a meltdown in a figure of authority. "Well, I think it would . . . uh . . . be okay if you parked here for a few minutes," said the guard. "In fact, I'll personally keep an eye on your car to make sure nobody tickets it. You run on and do your business." Beau thanked him profusely, and we were able to complete our mission without getting wet. In fact, as we were leaving, the guard moved some wooden barriers so that we could go out a special exit. True service equals meltdown. Beau told the guard that we knew he was the boss, and the boss made a decision to serve us. The circle was complete.

I think we sorely underestimate the heart of God. We have a creator who delights in giving us the kingdom, so as leaders we should do our utmost to serve those placed in our kingdom. We should give them good things . . . with pleasure. Jesus said, "I always do what God asks me to do."[114] He also said, "God always does what I ask him to do."[115] What you have here is a portrait of the Godhead serving one another.

In fact, Jesus even served food. The Bible tells about how he sent his people on a mission and when they returned he said, "Come, you must be tired. I've prepared a picnic for you."[116] After he first returned from the dead, he made a picnic on the shore, just waiting for the disciples to recognize him. He did not notify the media, nor did he need any special effects. He just decided to serve another meal.

So many Bible stories show God, the ultimate leader, preparing banquets, throwing parties, and bringing out the best wine to celebrate the return of an errant child. Bible stories also tell about leaders like the Good Samaritan who took time out from his mission to assist a battered enemy on the road and who said, "Anything else that this man needs, put on my account."[117]

Some wise elders advised a young king with these words: "If you love this people, *and serve them*, and speak kind words to them, they will love you and follow you forever."[118]

Jesus served them.

Question

What are the ways that you truly serve your people?

Question

Think of ten more ways you could serve them.

He Loved Them

In the Gospels of Matthew, Mark, Luke, and John, the authors often describe people as those Jesus *loved*. When Jesus encountered the rich young ruler, he looked at him and *loved* him. Another staff member describes a scene in which Jesus went to see Lazarus, the man he *loved*. John the disciple was described as someone Jesus *loved*. In his final message Jesus declared that he *loved* his staff as much as his own Father loved him and that he came to show the people how to love each other. As the saying goes, "When everything is said and done, only love will last."[119]

Love is the infrastructure of everything and anything

worthwhile. If someone with X-ray vision looked for love in your endeavors, what would they see? Where would they find the love? Some companies are held together only by paychecks; and in some companies, the love is so strong that people would pay just to be part of them. What kind of company is yours?

Jesus spoke for three years on everything from how not to swallow a camel to how to become the greatest of all. Yet ultimately he summarized his teaching in one sentence: "Love God with all your heart and mind and soul and strength, and your neighbor as yourself."[120] Jesus could lead people because, quite simply, he loved them.

There is a legend about John, the staff member Jesus loved, being quizzed again and again by eager young converts regarding heavenly principles. In a packed meeting hall, John said to the crowd, "Little children, love one another."[121] "That's great, John, but how do we heal the sick like he did?" asked an eager young man. John stood up again and said, "Little children, love one another." "Okay, John, we get the point, but how can we become *truly* great leaders?" asked the crowd. John rose up again and said quietly, "Little children, love one another."

Suppose the following was a page in your personal policy manual: I will be patient and kind . . . never envious or boastful or rude. I will not seek my own way nor be easily provoked. I will rejoice in the truth and will always seek out the best in others. I will hope for all things, believe

STRENGTH OF RELATIONSHIPS

in all things, bear all things, and endure all things.[122] Recessions may come and go, economies and market conditions may rise and fall, but I will never fail, for love is my guiding light, and ultimately, love knows all.

Jesus knew his staff would ultimately come back to him.

Because he loved them.

Question

If your staff members were asked to describe your feelings for them, whom would they say you loved?

Question

On what actions of yours would they base their answer?

Question

What are three new ways you can show your love for your staff?

He Defended Them

A common saying in business is: The customer is always right. In the case of management, it should be: Your staff is always right . . . at least as far as the public is concerned.

The story that brings this to mind is the one in which the scribes and the Pharisees came to Jesus and told him to rebuke his staffers because they were eating wheat on the Sabbath.[123] Clearly, Jesus knew the rules; and clearly, the staff was breaking them. However, instead of turning and rebuking his errant crew, he turned to the scribes and the Pharisees. "You strain at a gnat and swallow a camel,"[124] he told them in no uncertain terms and shamed them into silence for their criticism. Jesus defended his staff in front of the public.

In another instance, a woman accused of adultery was dragged before him. Again, someone had clearly broken the law. Jesus could have won the scribes' approval by upholding their sense of righteousness. Instead, he asked the people who were without sin to throw the first stone at her. When the trembling woman looked up at him, he said, "Where are your accusers?" She said, "They are gone." He said, "Neither do I accuse you. Go in peace."[125] Some people say this is the same woman who later sold everything she had to help support Jesus in his work. He had defended her.

And then there is the case of his own cousin, John. John saw the clouds open up and heard the voice from heaven saying "This is my beloved son." John had been thrown into prison and there began to doubt. He became so depressed and confused that he even sent someone to ask Jesus, "Are you sure you're who you say you are?" This messenger asked the question of Jesus in public, and I'm sure a hush fell over the crowd. John the Baptist was doubting the very man he had baptized. But Jesus quickly defended John, telling the crowd that John was one of the finest people who had ever lived. He told the messenger to go tell John what he had seen and heard. Nowhere did

Jesus attempt to discredit even this doubting staffer, despite the anger and humiliation he may have felt. Instead he defended him.[126]

When people work toward a goal, they are going to make mistakes . . . sometimes big ones. But considering that these people are the ones who must carry on the work if and when you are gone, with whom do you want to build loyalty? A critic who comes and goes? Or a staffer who might otherwise stay and go on to make you proud one day?

This situation happened at a women's resource center when we launched an ambitious crusade to correct a law that was allowing people to have family members institutionalized with only one physician's signature. Several prominent men in the community were abusing this law by having wives who were divorcing them signed into the county mental hospital by their golf-buddy physicians. "It usually happens on Fridays," the sheriff complacently told us. "That way the gals can't get out until Monday." We brought this situation to the attention of the media, which ran a two-part investigative series.

However, one of the prominent men complained to a board member, who complained to the executive director, who at this time was not committed to her staff. She promised publicly to have her staff members reprimanded, fearing that these prominent people might cut off contributions to the center.

The executive director played politics and as a result

lost three of her finest staff members. In fact, this executive director never did bond with her staff, and ultimately the center dwindled down to a staff of two: herself and one volunteer. Nothing of much controversy or significance was accomplished after that, as the director spent most of her time searching for funds for a program that had no heart — or guts.

In simple terms, you will have to sweat sometimes in order to have staff members worth any salt, and part of that sweat will result from defending them from others . . . sometimes others with power.

Jesus defended them.

Question

Have you ever rebuked or embarrassed a staff member in public? How do you think it made them feel?

Question

How can you defend your staff on a day-to-day basis?

Question

List three times that you had to make a choice to defend or reprimand one of your staff members. What were the consequences?

He Gave Them
<u>Authority</u>

❧

If someone was to tally the number of human hours wasted in business by people trying to accomplish objectives without being given the authority to do so, we would all be appalled. I personally have experienced working with people who were unprepared to make a decision, not knowing whether they could or not. I have seen groups draw up glorious plans of action to present to boards that meet twice a year and have ten minutes to discuss each project. The answer is usually "Let's table it until next time." Since the people who drew up the plans were not given the authority to implement them, the plans remained just that — plans that were destined to die in committee.

The board's reluctance to grant these people authority is understandable. The board's power would be diluted. Also, committees would rather not take action, because taking action means making decisions, and making decisions is painful. One study shows that people equate making a decision with the same stress level as being given a shot.

Jesus gave his staffers authority to act in his name even before they seemed ready for it. When he first sent them out with this newfound authority to heal the sick and raise the dead, he must have paced by the sea wondering what they were going to come back with. Sure enough, they came back with tales of success, but also stories about how they sometimes couldn't quite get it. Jesus' response was classic. "Oh, faithless and perverse generation, how long must I suffer thee?"[127]

Yet he gave them authority, and eventually they became quite good at carrying out the mission. By giving them authority to act, he was delegating power. There was much work to be done that he could not humanly or even divinely do without them. "The fields are ripe for harvest, but the workers are few."[128] So he took the workers he did have and gave them authority.

Jesus also gave his staffers clear instructions on what to do with this authority: Heal the sick and raise the dead. He even told them what they were to wear and whom to talk to.[129] He did not just send them out without a plan.

Delegation of authority requires a tremendous amount of trust. Perhaps that is why there are so many confused employees, because there are so many fearful people at the top. If leaders operate out of fear, they cannot delegate. A leader who does not delegate will end up with a group of yes people who will ultimately lead to his or her demise.

Leaders must share information and the subsequent authority that goes with it. This way they can empower others to do the right thing in ways that will offer fulfillment, not only on an individual level, but on a global basis as well. To grant authority is to leverage one's gifts.

Jesus gave them authority.

Question

How much authority do you give your staff members?

Question

What guidelines have you given your staffers about what they can and cannot do?

Question

What areas of authority have you not shared with them yet? Why?

He Played
with Them

One of the strictest rules in the military is that officers should not mingle with the noncommissioned officers. Some management books say that if you get too close to your employees, they will take advantage of you. "Good fences make good neighbors," wrote Robert Frost. We are a species obsessed with boundaries.

Jesus, the Omega leader, had no boundaries as far as his group was concerned. Kids ran up to hug him. His staff had to force crowds to leave him late at night so he could rest. Everyone wanted him to come to their parties. Jesus played with his people. He surely reflected joy and laughter or people would not have flocked to him so.

Jesus was the ultimate charismatic leader, and most charismatic personalities have a healthy sense of humor. (People who don't think God has a sense of humor have never seriously studied a kangaroo.) Although there are few representations of Jesus laughing, he surely must have spent a great deal of time doing so. He must have been touched and amused by the antics of his young enthusiastic staff. "Hold on, Jesus, I'll be right there!" Peter might have yelled as he stepped onto the water and then sank like a stone. The Zebedee brothers probably caused more than one snicker as they argued about who was going to be first in the kingdom and then were left behind when the group made an unexpected right turn into the garden.

Jesus went to parties. He sang songs with people and told them story after story about the land he knew. He made them picnics on the shore. He held their children. He enjoyed watching their faces as one loaf of bread turned into 3 and then 300 and then 3,000. He was so intimately involved with his staff that he even healed an ailing mother-in-law at one of the parties. He probably danced a step or two of joy when the lame man threw down his crutches and ran up to hug him.

Anyone who has been around circles of power and influence knows that most deals are made on the golf course or outlined on cocktail napkins over drinks or dinner. I have seen many eager leaders trying to bring others to the conference table, instead of to the party. They would be better off playing with their clients first.

The world is bursting with joy. Jesus must have embodied that or he could not have been who he said he was. A transparent leader is full of joy, because nothing is hidden. Leaders who share their spontaneity and joy build love and loyalty. Bonding occurs when defenses are down, and nowhere are people more open to love than when they are playing.

Jesus played with them.

Question

When was the last time you and your staff members played together?

Question

When was the last time you laughed with them?

Question

Are you trying to bring your people to the table or to the party?

He Harbored
Only Goodwill

James Autrey, in his book *For Love and Profit*, credits one of his staff members with teaching him a key leadership principle: the presumption of goodwill. He states that he watched her bring calm to warring parties and develop creative solutions to problems between people by opening her meetings with this sentence: "Now, let's presume that everyone here has goodwill toward each other, and proceed from there." Jesus presumed the best about people . . . even when they nailed him to the cross.

He called us lambs and children — never sinning worms. I walked out of a church once because the preacher kept saying that we were sinning worms. Now I ask you, how does a worm sin? Besides, I was made in the image of God. Who was that preacher to tell me I am unworthy of God's love?

Jesus presumed the best in us. He saw us as future kings and queens and was quick to excuse and forgive our lesser acts, knowing we were capable of so much more. "Yes, Peter. You denied me. But you will be my Rock. Yes, Mary, you've had men who weren't your husband. But you are capable of great love."

Since he saw the best in us, he could handle the worst in us. He knew that with divine help and a willingness on our part, everything could be made right. The wounds in his hands would heal.

"Father, forgive them. For they know not what they do."[130] This statement is like a blanket of mercy thrown over our most fearful deed. We were not the best to him, but he believed we wanted to be. He said so with his dying breath. That is why he was such a great negotiator on our behalf. He believed that ultimately we could make the angels sing and God truly proud.

Jesus harbored only goodwill.

Question

What would change in your dealings with people if you presumed only their goodwill?

Question

Does your point of view affect your followers?
How?

He Gave Them
Something Tangible
to Remember Him By

From a material aspect, Jesus left his people with little more than memories. The only possession he had at his death was his robe, which ended up being bartered for by the Roman soldiers.

Yet Jesus did give his people something tangible to remember him by: the Last Supper. This was a ritual of communion based on his words "Every time you eat this bread and drink this wine, remember me."[131] He gave them a beautiful parting memory that they could touch and taste and feel.

Human nature encourages us to have bonding rituals that help us feel closer to others and like part of a team.

An obvious example of this is our sports leagues. The players on the field have huddles, back slapping, and bear hugs. There is almost as much physical contact going on in the stands. Animal hoots, the Wave, hugging, high fives, and hot dogs are all part of the way we make each other feel close at arena events. We like the tangible things that accompany the highs and lows of winning and losing . . . or just playing the game.

I recently learned that most people approach horses the wrong way. Rather than an outstretched hand or a friendly pat on the neck, horses respond more to someone who breathes slowly and deeply into their nostrils so that they can capture the essence of that person's smell. This is, in fact, how horses greet and bond with each other. It is their ritual.

Too many companies have sterile atmospheres with look-alike desks and people with expressionless faces going through monotonous motions. I wonder if anyone at the top has tried to bond with these people. Instead of walking by and patting them on the back, CEOs should get "nostril to nostril" with them and take the time to "breathe in their world" as much as they want them to live and breathe theirs.

How a ritual applies to business is up to each leader or manager to decide. In our company we have a ritual called "the dance of joy." We do this spontaneously when something wonderful happens (like a check comes in) or

STRENGTH OF RELATIONSHIPS

when an idea or piece of copy seems unusually inspired. We grab the closest person and link arms. After a few high kicks and a good laugh, we go back to what we were doing.

One day I noticed that as our secretary was talking on the phone, her fingers were doing little leaps and twirls. When I asked her later what the hand movements were all about, she explained, "I was doing a mini-dance of joy because Mr. Big Wig returned my call."

Employees will come and go in even the best of worlds. There will be days when you feel like doing the march of doom instead of the dance of joy. Not too long ago I found myself raising my voice at one of our "beloved" employees. The next afternoon, when things had cooled off, we sat in my office and talked about what both of us could do to help one another more. This conversation went on from four until six in the evening. Both of us quietly revealed our concerns, fears, and hopes for the future. As we were sitting there I noticed that the light outside had changed. It had gone from a harsh afternoon yellow to a peaceful golden glow. We both left the meeting feeling renewed. We had bonded again. As we were leaving, the employee said, "That was the most uninterrupted time I've had with you since I started working here."

Sometimes an important bonding ritual can be just sitting quietly with a staff member, until the light inside turns from a harsh yellow into a deep, rich gold. Later I gave her a little golden key—to symbolize all the new doors that were being opened for us.

Jesus understood the need for people to have tangible things to remember him by. It was his ultimate gift to his staff—bread and wine representing tears and all the laughter.

He gave them something tangible to remember him by.

Question
What are some of the bonding rituals or activities in your group?

Question
Are these rituals official or unofficial?

Question
What tangible things have you given your people to remember you by?

He Wanted

to Take

Everyone to the Top

Jesus hated to eat alone. Witness the fact that he used words like "whosoever will" as the criterion for the mailing list to the banquet. His last request was that his entire staff could go to heaven with him. He invited the thief dying on the cross to join him in Paradise.

Let's face it. We need each other. Tarzan would have been a very boring story without Jane, Boy, and Cheetah. And anyone who claims to be a self-made man or woman doesn't know much about biology. Yet every day there are people — managers and leaders — who try to climb their way to the top using other people as their stepladder.

A classic example of this attitude took place in a

meeting I attended where Jim, an executive director of a 30,000-member organization, refused to cooperate with our company in a joint venture unless he could have total control of the project. Jim kept emphasizing that his organization would have final control on everything from copy, to creativity, to concept, to implementation. "Then why would you need us?" I asked. Our company had already come up with the copy, concept, and creativity, and was simply offering Jim's organization a piece of the implementation. "W-well," he stammered. "I don't know what we would need you for. I guess to give us ideas. But again I emphasize that I would have absolute, final, and total control." He leaned forward intently, stabbing his finger in the air at me, and said, "This project would be *my* baby." I leaned forward, having come to the realization that I didn't want to work with him anyway, and said, "Jim, may I remind you that it takes two people to make a baby?"

Unfortunately, this was just one example of the attitude that prevailed in that organization. If it did not come from Jim, it was not going to be. Jim was determined to stay at the top. (One year later Jim was relieved of his command. The new executive director invited me in as Jim was leaving. We literally crossed paths at the door.)

In Chicago there is a multimillionaire who persists in working eighteen hours a day developing his people. When asked why he works so hard, since he has already made his millions, he said, "Because my goal is to help create *more* millionaires out of this company." Motivation runs high in his office. People feel empowered and energized. Cynics might say it is the promise of gold. I say that his employees also are responding to the promise of loving guidance and support.

Jesus said "I give you my name. Use it."

He wanted to take as many people to the top with him as possible.

Question
How many people do you intend to take with you on the road to success?

Question
Does your action plan include those people?

Question
Are they aware of it?

He Saw Them as
God's Gifts to Him

In his final recorded prayer on earth, Jesus said, "These people were your gifts to me."[132] They were not projects to be completed. Sinners to be changed. Fools to be corrected. Worms to be transformed. Corporate pawns to be maneuvered until the plan was in place. They were gifts to him.

Jesus looked at Peter and said, "Peter, you were God's gift to me." He looked at John and said, "John, you were God's gift to me." He looked at Mary and said, "Mary, you were God's gift to me." He knew that God would not give him something that was not intrinsically good.

People were the gifts that made God's son happy. Jesus enjoyed their company. They made him feel loved. In fact, they made him so happy that Jesus' final request before his departure was that they might all be together again in heaven. He taught them and he trained them, but his joy did not come from the end result. It came from the process and from their companionship.

Your staff members may or may not execute the plans that you have so brilliantly set before them. If you are an Omega leader, chances are good that they will. However, you must never forget that these people are, most of all, someone's greatest gifts to you. Enjoy them. Cherish them. Defend them. Relish them.

To shepherd a flock of butterflies, one must stand there in delight.

Jesus saw them as God's gifts to him.

Question
Do you believe your staff members are God's gifts to you?

Question
Do you treat them accordingly?

Question
List one aspect about each staff member that

shows she or he was hand-picked for your greatest *needs*.

Question

List one aspect about each staff member that shows he or she was hand-picked for your greatest *joy*.

He Loved Them
to the End

~∂~

We live in a world where the words "till death do us part" have meaning for only half of the couples who recite them with all the sincerity they can muster. We live in a world where the needs and potential of the human heart have not changed.

At a board meeting a few years ago, I broke the number-one cardinal rule for women. I cried. I was frustrated at some of the slow responses and outright hostilities I had encountered while trying to implement the changes that we had all decided were needed. In front of fourteen board members, I cried. Later they each rose to comfort me and apologize for their behavior. "We weren't sure we could trust you," they said. "Now we understand that you truly care." My crying broke the dam of their distancing behavior.

Businesses cannot operate without caring. Companies that exude customer service are really saying that they see who you are and care about you as a person. I tell doctors in my marketing seminars (only half jokingly) that if they would send out flowers and get-well cards to their patients, they would not need malpractice insurance. People do not sue someone they feel really cares about them. (Unless they live in California.)

When I looked up the phrase "Jesus looked at the young man, and looking at him, loved him,"[133] I first thought it must have been about John or Peter. But the reference, which I had remembered just for the sheer poetry of it, was actually about the rich young ruler who stood eagerly facing Jesus and asked, "What must I do to enter the kingdom of heaven?" "Loose your ties to your possessions and follow me" was Jesus' reply. Yet the young man turned his head and walked away. Having measured the cost, he decided it was too dear.

The interesting thing about this story is that Jesus loved the young man even as he walked away. He did not withdraw his love because the young man did not meet his quota or jump on the bandwagon. This was one man who walked away and yet Jesus still loved him.

I want to be like that. To still love the clients who do not renew contracts. To still love the people I have had to fire and the ones who have had to fire me.

A recent book about a multimillionaire written by a disgruntled employee comes to mind. The multimillionaire supposedly dismissed the book's author with the comment "He was never that important to us anyway." Perhaps that kind of attitude is why the employee left and wrote a scathing book.

Jesus never slammed a door or burned a bridge. He said, "Just knock on the door and I'll open it."[134] He meant any time, any place. He would be there. No matter how long someone had been gone or what she or he had said on the way out. He promised to be there.

Every door is built with hinges . . . perhaps for eternal reasons. As a carpenter, Jesus must have built a lot of doors in his Father's mansion. He knew that doors once shut could again be opened. Each of his staff members failed him, especially when he needed them most. Yet . . .

"Having loved his own who were in the world he loved them to the end."[135]

Question

Have you made a commitment to love your people no matter what?

Question

Have you put your trust in love even when there are separations?

Question

Has there been a time when you opened a door to another person that had previously been shut?

He Saw Them
as His Greatest
Accomplishment

"It is in them I am glorified."[136]

The more I work with the concept of Jesus as a CEO, the more amazed I am at this powerful, divinely energized leader's priorities. For example, in his final summary to God in John 17, Jesus did not relate even one miracle that he performed. His summary did not read:

> Dear Chairman of the Board,
>
> I have completed my task here by doing the following:
>
> 1. Raising the dead (little girl and Lazarus).
>
> 2. Turning water into wine (at wedding feast).
>
> 3. Multiplying the loaves and fishes (on numerous occasions).
>
> 4. Reducing the number of those on sick leave throughout my territory.

He did not say "I've left construction of the temple in capable hands and it should be finished by May." Nor did he say "I've doubled the number of your recruits here and you will note offerings are up in three locations." Instead, he listed his people as his greatest accomplishment. His summary read:

> Dear Chairman of the Board,
>
> As proof of my good work here, I present to you Peter, James, John, Mary, Mary Magdalene, and Martha . . . completed in love.
>
> Jesus

I wrote this brief eulogy for a dear friend's father who died last May.

A beautiful man went to heaven last night.
God filled his heart with generosity
and he in turn poured it out on us.
A quick wit . . . a lover of poetry,
he taught us all he knew of love.
It is up to us now to live it.

We could say the same thing about Jesus. Here was a man who was a cultural phenomenon, who caused spiritual and political upheaval everywhere he went, and who changed people's lives every time he opened his mouth. For all of that, the only tangible thing he left behind was one tattered garment . . . and one Peter, one James, one John, one Mary, one Mary Magdalene, and one Martha.

These people were also the only "trophies" he asked to take with him into Paradise.

What fine work he did, this carpenter of human souls. He saw people as his greatest accomplishment and in so doing built them a table to last.

Jesus saw them as his greatest accomplishment.

Question

What (or who) would you consider as your greatest accomplishments?

Question

What actions would you change if loving God and your people, not the bottom line, became your highest priority?

He Knew That
Nobody Wins
Until We All Do

❧

A speaker from Dallas, Texas, recently shared this story with members of the National Speakers Association. One young man, set to run in a one hundred meter race in the Special Olympics, had trained for months and months. But when the gun finally sounded and he leaped out in front of the rest, it seems the excitement of the race overcame him. Each foot went in different directions, and the well-meaning athlete came tumbling down right in front of the starting block. The other racers, each as eager as he was to compete in this great event, nevertheless stopped running their own race and turned back to help him. The crowd came to their feet as his competitors lovingly lifted him up and then walked arm in arm across the finish line together.

These runners in the Special Olympics made me think of Jesus and his set of rules. I thought about him choosing to tell the story about the shepherd who cannot rest as long as even one sheep is still missing, despite the ninety-nine of them which aren't . . . about a father who is waiting on the road, watching for his lost son to come home, even though he has one son who is serving him ably and well . . . about a king holding a banquet, who will not start serving dinner until every place is filled at the Great Table. . . .

And I wonder what this world would be like if we played by that rule: that nobody wins until we all do.

Then the people who crossed the finish line first would be motivated to turn back to help the other, less able ones across. I recently read that authorities found the arsonist who destroyed the barn of an Amish farmer. It was actually an Amish youth, intent upon rebellion, who had lit the blaze. When the press asked the farmer what punishment he thought the boy deserved, the man shook his head and with tears in his eyes said, "It is we who have failed him somehow. I say 'Come home, son, and let's talk.' " All their successful crops meant nothing if somehow the system had failed a youth.

Associated Press recently carried this story. "Recently, retired doctors hoping to narrow the gap between rich and poor at plush Hilton Head Island have set up a free clinic for the maids, gardeners, waitresses, and others who make the place work. 'The health care system on this island was geared to the wealthy,' said Dr. Jack McConnell, who came up with the idea. 'But if a town leaves behind a portion of its citizens it will never be a true community.'"

Dan Shaughnessy, a friend who sold a successful consulting practice in Washington, D.C., to use his talents in heading an international relief effort called Project Concern, understands this concept. Lori DeForti, the young San Diego artist who won $11,000 worth of billboard space in a contest and then used it to spotlight other aspiring artists, understands this concept. The women in Boston who find time out of their busy careers to individually mentor unwed mothers understand this concept. Mother Teresa and AIDS volunteers and the host of saints and angels among us understand this concept.

Nobody wins until we all do.

Question

How many of your activities are predicated on "getting ahead"?

Question

How and when have you turned back to help someone else cross the finish line?

APPENDIX

Affirmations

for Leaders

- I proudly say I AM, knowing clearly my strengths and God-given talents. I repeat my strengths to myself often, knowing my words are my wardrobe.

- I have learned in my own wilderness what my strengths are. I use "desert times" to get clearer on my calling and my true goals.

- I am clear about my mission. I spend my time working on and accomplishing what is deepest and truest and most inspiring.

- I shape my own destiny. What I believe, I become. What I believe, I can do.

- What I say and ask for is accomplished for me in amazing ways and with amazing speed.

- I keep in constant contact with my Higher Power, knowing that I need added insight to see the road up ahead.

- I do the difficult things. I accomplish difficult and challenging tasks with strength and resolve, knowing that these jumps are placed in the arena for my training and strengthening.

- I do not need or seek others' approval. I am internally connected to my Higher Power and listen to the still, small voice that alone knows my best path.

- I commit my passion to my cause, knowing that passion is the power that creates new life, new joys, and new accomplishments for myself and others.

- I see things differently and am always willing to look at situations in new and enlivening ways.

- I behold others, taking time to be centered and to embrace them in each holy moment.

- I am aware that only God knows the total plan and that I am a part of it. What the Higher Power asks me to do, I do willingly.

- I urge myself and others on, unwilling to settle for less than the highest to which I am called.

- I sleep well at night, knowing that each of us is called to and capable of making our own choices.

- It is okay for me to hold others accountable for their own actions and the consequences of those actions, whatever they may be.

- I empower others through my example. I agree that masculine and feminine energy have equal rights and responsibilities.

- I quit whining and start walking, taking God's power in every situation.

- I spend lots of time with my staff, knowing that life, love, and laughter are learned by osmosis.

- I always convey to others my highest thoughts or feelings about any situation.

- I acknowledge others in public and in private. I see praise as being the number-one priority on everybody's paycheck.

- I release and forgive others, knowing that what is loosed on earth will be loosed in heaven. I aim to soar. I release others so that I myself can fly.

- I judge no one, knowing that judging others causes major energy leaks in my life. Judging others is not in my job description. When I judge others, I am automatically out of bounds and out of tune . . . especially with myself. I let a Higher Power deal with others' lives.

- I pray for others, carrying them like inscriptions day and night upon my heart. I seek their welfare and their good. I light candles for them daily in the quiet of my mind.

- I see my work with people as being my greatest joy, my greatest gift, and my greatest accomplishment.

- I see others as God's gift to me.

- I am open to others and their ideas. I know that others may have parts of the puzzle that are missing for me. I acknowledge their contributions openly and freely. I give them the credit that is their due.

- I am a transparent leader. I know my strength is in my openness and honesty with others.

- I believe in others. I always seek and believe in their good. I defend others, for when a sparrow falls, I, too, fall. We are all of one relation.

- I give others authority, knowing that by doing so

I am leveraging my gifts and influence and that I am empowering them to spread more good.

- I serve others, knowing that service is a circle: When I serve others, I, too, shall be served.

- I treat everyone as my equal. We are all kings and queens of empires. I respect the royalty in others, knowing that no matter what appearances may be, we are each royalty.

- I am constantly in a state of celebration. I see life as an opportunity to celebrate. I keep joy handy for any occasion. I share my cup with others.

- I see everything as being alive.

- I have a plan. I spend quality time daily developing and implementing my plan. I do not let others distract me or allow busyness to delude me.

- I reach out and touch the fragile things. I am aware of the fragile things in others. I find ways to nourish and nurture and make time for the delicate things in life. I look for the flowers along the freeway. I take the slow road sometimes.

- I call the question. I am eager and willing to make decisions and to take action. I believe and know that the truth will set me — and others — free.

- I know that fears may always be with me. I feel the fear and do it anyway. I plant my seeds even when there are clouds in the sky.

- I review and update my resources daily. I know that I have command of all that I see. I know that if I need something, I can ask and it will be given to me. I let the physics of unwavering faith do marvelous work for me.

- I take as many people to the top with me as possible.

- I look for ways to advance and enhance the life of everyone I know.

- I clearly define the rewards involved in any task . . . for myself and others. I keep sight of those rewards in difficult and challenging times.

- I branch out. I make my tent pegs firm and stretch out my banners freely. I widen the space of my tent. I know that I have beautiful territories ahead of me.

- I am now ten times bolder than I was yesterday. I do the bold things and take action. It is my destiny.

- I manage my life from the inside out. I keep the grass closest to me green. I take time to inform and educate and nurture those closest to me.

- I communicate clearly and simply. My *yes* means *yes*, and my *no* means *no*. I use two words when two words will do. My clarity is my power.

- I am willing to break ranks if my army is not marching. My calling is to be a leader, not a follower.

- I make the news, not just report it. Daily I go out and create positive news . . . for myself and others.

- I boil things down. I look for the true meaning. I do not waste time or energy carrying around unnecessary doubts or uncertainty.

- I am aware that God loves to play *surprise*. I offer myself as a resource and trust that the strength will come.

- I delight in others. I play with them and laugh with them and enjoy each moment. These are the pearls of life. They come one at a time.

- My word goes out and accomplishes that which I send it to do.

- I have a sense of destiny. I am destined to succeed.

- I do not despise the little things, knowing little seeds contain the potential for beauty and greatness.

- I trouble myself on God's behalf. I am not lazy about showing, through my actions, my love for God and others.

- I change the unit of measurement. I do not accept old standards that serve only to limit and repress my and other's greatness.

- I say "Why not me?" I am willing to accept God's greater challenges and blessings as they come.

- I let it go. I do not cling needlessly to people or projects that are causing me to lose my balance.

- I rise above it all. I look at things the way God looks at things — from an aerial view.

- I come to be a blessing. My goal is to bless others in multiple ways.

- I am a turnaround specialist. No task is too hard for me when I am working under Omega power.

- I know nobody wins until we all do. I am eagerly assisting others toward the greatest good.

Epilogue

Being someone who can agonize over how to end a simple business letter, the question of how to end this twenty year dream of *Jesus, CEO* has hovered over me for some time. Tonight, as I laid the final manuscript on my living room table, I noticed that it was surrounded by three of my favorite art objects — an angel, a flute player, and a spur. The answer suddenly became obvious. I pray that *Jesus, CEO*:

- will be like an angel, reminding us of heaven
- will be like a flute player, calling us to dance
- and will be like a spur, calling forth in each of us a renewed and higher effort toward the God who loves us all.

Laurie Beth Jones

A u t h o r ' s   N o t e s

Dear Reader,

I do not use the exact, literal, original Greek, Hebrew, or Aramaic text in the Scriptures I reference. I have sought to represent only the essence of the message. In fact, I was reluctant to cite chapter and verse of each scripture at all, having seen so many people escalate Bible quoting into some kind of Holy War. However, my mother insisted that these references be cited (and researched them all herself), so people "wouldn't think I made them up" and also so that others could study and interpret them for themselves.

I have studied so many versions of the Bible over the last twenty years that I cannot remember the exact wordings from each and every translation. My favorite is the *Jerusalem Bible*, so nine times out of ten, that is probably the one I am quoting.

My reference to Jesus as "he" in the lower case is in no way intended to be or to convey a diminuition of his Lordship or Divinity. It is merely an acknowledgment of a more contemporary writing style.

For me refer to God as "She" would unfortunately put this work beyond the boundaries of acceptance and understanding for too many people. We must search for an all-inclusive terminology.

My religious background is a conglomeration of Presbyterianism, Methodism, and ecumenical Christianity. My great-grandfather was a lay minister. My grandmother was part of a gospel singing group known as the Edwards Sisters who sang at temperance rallies throughout the Midwest. My mother once found her picture prominently displayed on the front page of our hometown newspaper with her eyes closed and her hands raised—the day after my father sighed, "Okay, Irene, go to those prayer meetings if you must. Just don't let anybody know about it."

I view the Bible as the record of an intense Love Story between us and God. And I believe that we can, through our actions, add to that Love Story every day.

Laurie Beth Jones

References

1. Mark 1:16, 3:14–18, Staff and followers.
2. Matthew 4:1–11, Wilderness experience.
3. John 4:25–26; Luke 22:27; John 8:23, 10:38, 10:36, 10:7, 10:11, 10:25, 13:13, 14:6; John 15:5, 18:37, 6:48, 6:51, 16:28, 10:7, 8:58; Matthew 11:29, 12:8, 28:20.
4. Exodus 3:14–15, God's name.
5. John 10:36, Declared himself to be the Son of God.
6. Isaiah 55:11, I declare.
7. John 7:29, I always do what pleases God.
8. John 11:42. God answers my prayers.
9. John 12:42–43, People's approval.
10. Matthew 10:14, Dust from your feet.
11. Matthew 7:6, Pearls before swine.
12. Luke 8:43–46, Who touched me?
13. Isaiah 50:7, And he set his face like a flint . . .
14. John 18:11, I will drink the cup.
15. John 11:41–42, He thanked God.
16. John 17:6–7, Thanked God for his staff.

17. John 6:9–13, One boy's lunch.
18. Matthew 18:19–20, Two or more.
19. John 14:2, I go to prepare a place for you.
20. Matthew 6:25–34, Why do you worry?
21. Genesis 1:26, Adam and Eve.
22. Genesis 13:17, All is yours. I give you.
23. John 5:45, I do not judge you.
24. John 21:21–22, Peter, what business is it of yours?
25. Luke 23:40–43, Thief on the cross.
26. Mark 9:17–27, Young boy with epilepsy.
27. Numbers 22:28, Balaam's ass speaks.
28. John 18:10, Peter cuts off guard's ear.
29. Matthew 21:12, Money changers.
30. Revelations 3:15, Hot as fire, cold as ice.
31. Kings 18:37–39, Elijah and Baal's prophets.
32. I Kings 2:9–14, Double dose of Elijah's spirit.
33. John 13:37–38, Can you really follow me?
34. Isaiah 32:8, Noble man.
35. II Samuel 16:5, 9, 10, Cursing David.
36. John 19:10–11, Authority from on high.
37. 2 Samuel 23:5, All in order.
38. Matthew 17:27, Fish, coin, taxes.
39. Matthew 21:2, Find the donkey.
40. John 8:14, I know where I came from.
41. John 19:11, No power over me.
42. I Corinthians 13:12, I will know.
43. Matthew 22:30, All are alive.
44. John 21:25, World could not contain the books.
45. John 5:15–17, My father goes on working.
46. John 19:26, John, Mary is your mother.
47. Matthew 9:24–25, She is not dead.
48. Mark 9:35–37, First, last; last, first.
49. I Samuel 17, David and Goliath.
50. John 1:45–46, Anything good out of Nazareth.
51. I Samuel 17:33–37, Burning heart.
52. Exodus 3:2–10, Burning bush.
53. Esther 2–8, Burning house.
54. Isaiah 54:2, Widen your tent.
55. Deuteronomy 11:24, Every inch of the ground.
56. Psalms 108:9, I throw my sandal over Edom.
57. Jeremiah 23:5, The branch of the Lord.
58. Matthew 22:37, Love God.
59. John 1:14, Word became flesh.
60. John 18:9, Let them go.

References

61. II Samuel 14:28–33, Set the fields on fire.
62. Matthew 26:6–13, Broken bottle of ointment.
63. Matthew 26:47–49, Judas betrayed him.
64. Matthew 4:19, Fishers of men.
65. John 4:13, Never be thirsty again.
66. Proverbs 29:18, No vision, perish.
67. Mark 10:21, Looking at him, loved him.
68. Hebrew 13:2, Entertained angels unaware.
69. Galations 3:28, All are equal in his sight.
70. Matthew 7:7–8, Ask and it shall be given.
71. Matthew 7:9–10, Be given a stone?
72. Genesis 2:19, That will be their name.
73. John 11:41, God always gives me what I ask.
74. Matthew 28:9–10, Resurrected appearance to women.
75. John 20:24–25, Thomas would not believe.
76. Luke 1:26–35, Young Mary.
77. Luke 8:3, Women supported Jesus and his staff.
78. Matthew 28:1–10, Women first to recognize resurrection.
79. Luke 24:13, Road to Emmaus.
80. Matthew 27:19, Pilate's wife.
81. Luke 17:20–21, The kingdom is within you.
82. Lord's Prayer, previously quoted.
83. Matthew 17:2; Mark 9:2–3; Luke 9:29, Transparent before them.
84. Proverbs 28:13, Cover and get punished, confess/mercy.
85. Matthew 16:17–18, On this rock.
86. Acts 11:1–18, Peter sent to the Gentiles.
87. John 10:10–11, Life abundantly.
88. Matthew 13:45–46, Pearl of great price.
89. Luke 22:61, Three times denied.
90. John 21: 15–17, Feed my sheep.
91. Exodus 20:7, Profane use of God's name; Deuteronomy 28:58–62, Plagues as punishment for irreverence.
92. I Chronicles 13:9, Uzzah touched the Ark and Yahweh struck him down.
93. Leviticus 21:17–21, Physical deformities.
94. Leviticus 15:19, Impurities.
95. Deuteronomy 34:10, Nobody but Moses got to talk to him.
96. Matthew 4:23, Teaching, healing, and preaching.
97. John 8:11, Go and sin no more.
98. John 6:5–9, How shall we feed all these people?

99. Matthew 18:18, Loose and bind.

100. Matthew 28:20, I am with you always.

101. John 13:14–15, Setting an example.

102. Exodus 28:15, Breastplate or *ephod*.

103. Isaiah 49:15–16, Person's name on the palm of his hand.

104. Luke 12:6–7, Hairs on your head.

105. Luke 3:22, My beloved son, I am pleased.

106. Luke 9:35, My beloved son, hear him.

107. Luke 19:2–5, Zacchaeus.

108. Mark 10:13–15, They were bringing children to him.

109. John 6:66–69, Are you too going to leave?

110. Matthew 26:38, Will you wait in the garden with me?

111. I Samuel 17:18–20, David and Jonathan.

112. Matthew 23:27, O Jerusalem.

113. John 11:35, Jesus wept.

114. John 7:29, I always do what God asks me to do.

115. John 11:42, God always hears my prayers.

116. John 21:9 – 13, He prepared a picnic for them.

117. Luke 10:35, Good Samaritan.

118. II Chronicles 10:7, If you love this people.

119. I Corinthians 13:13, Only love will last.

120. Matthew 22:36–39, Love God with all your heart.

121. I John 3:23, Little children, love one another.

122. I Corinthians 13:4–7, Patient and kind.

123. Mark 2:23, Eating wheat on the Sabbath.

124. Matthew 23:23, Gnat and camel.

125. John 8:3–7, 11: He drew in the sand.

126. Luke 7:18–20, 28, Cousin John doubts.

127. Matthew 18:17–18, Faithless and perverse generation.

128. Matthew 9:36–37, Fields are ripe.

129. Matthew 10:1–23, He gave them clear instructions.

130. Luke 23:33–34, Father, forgive.

131. Luke 22:19, Bread and wine.

132. John 17:6, These people were your gifts to me.

133. Mark 10:17–22, Looking at him, loved him.

134. Matthew 7:7–8, Just knock on the door.

135. John 13:1, Having loved his own.

136. John 17:9–10, It is in them I am glorified.

Enrollment Offer

If you would like information about upcoming seminars, retreats, speaking engagements, or consulting services, please send your name, address, company name, fax, and phone number to:

> The Jones Group
> 813 Summersong Court
> Encinitas, CA 92024
> (619)753-7251
> Fax (619)634-2707
> e-mail: laurie@lauriebethjones.com

Also, please feel free to send us your success stories using the Omega Management principles. We may publish these in upcoming newsletters or articles.

Acknowledgments

Since it is an Omega principle to publicly acknowledge others, I do not undertake this privilege lightly.

I feel a tremendous debt of gratitude to those who helped make this book possible.

Sandra Marleen Harrison, Ph.D., used part of her summer vacation to study my voluminous rough notes, and, with her feet propped up on my balcony, said, "Laurie, this work is as important as anything else you are doing. Finish it." Dominic Giambona came through with much-needed guidance and support at a critical turning point as Mary and I contemplated how to run an ad agency, navigate the California recession, and write a book about Jesus at the same time. Lawreve and Siegfried Widmar graciously and enthusiastically asked me to teach the principles at their first business conference. Renee Tepper and Karen Van Dyke urged me to present it at the San Diego Regional Women's Conference, where four hundred women rallied around the concept, giving us tremendous support for going forward. Cynthia Lee Hill lovingly edited the first draft, as well as encouraged me through all its various transformations. Becky Colgan, Shelly Hardy, Marta Meler, and Terri Whitehead spent countless hours typesetting and refining the manuscript. Dee Jones gave of her time and talents unsparingly in this book's birthing process.

Julie Castiglia, my phenomenal literary agent (who laughingly reminded me that her initials are "J. C.") hand-carried the proposal to numerous publishers during what happened to be one of New York City's worst heat waves, never doubting that it would find the perfect home. Bob Miller and my golden-voiced editor, Mary Ann Naples, championed the book at Hyperion, enthusiastically grasping the vision and working with me to hone it to its best possible form. Laurie Chittenden, Lisa Kitei, and Carol Perfumo at Hyperion also contributed greatly to the project.

My clients often have been a source of inspiration to me. Ken Creasman, CEO of Community Care of America, Inc., has given me incredible opportunities to both experience and demonstrate these principles in a corporation that is revolutionizing health care in rural America. The many fine physicians and staff at the American Academy of Osteopathy, and numerous osteopathic hospitals, colleges, and state associations have given me deep insights into the leadership skills of those who work in the exciting and challenging arena of health care. Bill Dowdy and Bernie Krupa at ServiceMaster gave me valuable confirmation regarding the practicality of harnessing spirituality in the business world. Rinaldo Brutoco introduced me to the World Business Academy, and to others who are seeking and creating new paradigms in business. George Marks and Mary Ellen Drummond appeared like angels when I needed them. Tino Ballesteros, Arturo Bañuelos, Wendy Craig-Purcell, Sam Faraone, Don Forsman, Marcia Geckler, Renee Geiger, and Beth Harrington are ministers who each encouraged and inspired me in special and timely ways. Colene Absalom and Willy Bonkers fed me and kept me laughing during many long hot days of writing out at Gold Rock Ranch.

I am keenly aware that every person who touches a life, helps shape it. People who have been like shade trees and canteens for me along my journey include: Sylvia Alcantar, Nancy Borrettloiselle, Clyde and Dulce Boyer, Sandra Carrillo, Jeffrey D. Cohen, Sandy Cooper, Fred Davis, Jo Ann Dempsey, Dennis Deniger, Stephen Dunn, Rita Esparaza, Ron Estep, Bill Filippone, Diane Gardner, Carla Gasway, Dick Gingery, Phil Greening, Frenchie Guajardo, Arnie Hammer, Marilyn Hall Day, Mary Ann Higgins, Harry Lee Hudspeth, Dee Jibillian, Gail Kingsbury, Bill Krystopowicz, Luann Linquist, Cinda Lucas, Mary Marcdante, Martine Marcello, Leland Marple, Linda Marraro, Nanci McGraw, Jose Melendez, Phyllis Michel, Mona Moon, Ayde Nieto, John Purcell, Richard Rierdan, DJ Ryan, Sally Scaman, Mary Scott, Dan and Judy Shaughnessy, Mary Sheldon, Rudy and Rose Ann Smith, Edgar Songy, Don Stadelli, Tom and Jan Sterrett, Margie Thomas, Pat Uri, Anne Westrope, Ginita Wall, and Sumner Walz.

My work with the osteopathic profession has gifted me with a number of talented physicians and associates as friends. Among them are: David Abend, Alan and Honey Becker, John Bowling, Barbara Briner, Boyd Buser, Mark Cantieri, Constance Cashen, Isabelle Chappello, Tony Chila, Joe Colturi, Norval Copeland, Eileen DiGiovanna, Eric and Robin Dolgin, Mary Eckert, George Eistetter, Joe Ferguson, Viola Frymann, John Goodrich, Ann Habenicht, Ray Hruby, Bob Jones, John Jones, Marty and Mitch Kasovac, William and Mike Kuchera, David Kushner, Barbara Ross Lee, Judy Lewis, Stan Louie, John McHugh, Jill Ellen McKee, James Murphy, Steve Noone, Judy O'Connell, Ted Podleski, Lisa Rader, Randy and Judy Roulier, Margaret and Harry Royson, Jay Sandelin, Roger Spoelman, Karen Steele, Melicien A. Tettambel, Mary Theodoras, Rick Vincent, Harlan Wright, Bill Wyatt, and Herb and Terry Yates.

Other friends who have encouraged and helped me

include: Tony Alessandra, Camille Ashcraft, Bob Baker, David Brown, David Cowan, Sheryl Dacso, Bob Di-Baudo, Christine Elliott, Jolene Fullerton, Nancy Gardner, Nancy Haller, Mary Ellen Hamilton, Ben Ivey, Bennie, Wade, and Tara Ivey, Marion Keller, Mickey and Charlene Kesselman, Joanne Kezas, Charles and Rebecca Lawrence, Steve Leatherwood, Vicky Ledet, Sari Love, Richard Marks, Dale Martin, Lorrie McGrath, Pam Means, Susanna Palomares, Linda Pinson, Wayne Pitchard, Jenni Prisk, Sarah Race, Robert Rankin, Joel and Patti Ray, John and Bonnie Rush, Harold Ryan, Mike Scott, Lynn Siebrandt, Jody Simms, Susan Smith, Maureen Sweeney, Helene Theodoras, Priscilla Trowbridge, Mike Vandergreen, Debbie Voltura, Diane White, and Jim Williams.

I owe a career full of gratitude to Pearl Crouch, my high school journalism teacher, who believed wholeheartedly in the giftedness of her students. Linda Sterrett Marple has been such a loving and long-standing believer in me that her friendship calls for a book in itself. Beau Black and Deborah Kelly Owens validated and treasured my writing throughout my high school years.

My sister, Kathy Jones Ivey, is one of the kindest and funniest people alive, and my witty, loving, and supportive brother, Joe Jones, helped create and then had to endure an atmosphere of puns and word games around the family table. If there is a "pun-free" reward zone in heaven, these two have certainly earned it. Thank you for loving me all these years.

An inmeasurable thank you goes to my mother, Irene Jones, for lullabies and art lessons and belief in the feminine. Catherine Calhoun, one of the nation's wisest and brightest organizational development consultants, first got me excited about the potential for spiritual service in business settings. Without her profound influence, I know I would not have seen these principles come alive.

And finally, to Jesus, my CEO, who laughs with, listens, and whispers to me still, my thanks. I pray you find this work worthy of your name.

Laurie Beth Jones

About the Author

Laurie Beth Jones is president and founder of The Jones Group, an advertising, marketing, and business development firm whose mission is "To recognize, promote and inspire divine excellence." With her partner Mary Ellen Dempsey, and a team of highly energized experts, they specialize in health care marketing.

Listed in the International *Who's Who*, Laurie is a former president of the El Paso Chapter of American Women in Radio and Television, was among the first Most Notable Women of Texas, was named an Outstanding West Texas Scholar, and is an alumna of Leadership El Paso and Lead San Diego. She has won numerous awards in design, copywriting, poetry, speech, and racquetball.

She conceived the idea for *Jesus, CEO* while she was living in the mountains of New Mexico and listening to the forest with her brown dog, Shiloh. She has authored two musicals, more than two hundred songs, several books of poetry, and is still "Profoundly excited by the spiritual quest."